A BARTHOLOMEW MAP AND GUIDE

WALK THE LAKES AGAIN

38 EASY WALKS
Selected and described by John Parker

John Bartholome
Edinburg

C000131831

British Library Cataloguing in Publication Data
Parker, John, *1925*
    Walk the lakes again: easy walks.-(A
    Bartholomew map and guide)
    1. Lake District (England) - Description and
    travel - Guide-books
    I. Title
    914.27'804858   DA670.L1
    ISBN 0 7028 0724 9

Published and Printed in Scotland
by John Bartholomew & Son Ltd.,
Duncan Street, Edinburgh EH9 1TA

Text copyright © John Parker 1985
Maps copyright © John Bartholomew & Son Ltd. 1985

ISBN 0 7028 0724 9

The physical landscape of Britain is changing all the time e.g. as new
tracks are made, hedges grubbed up and fields amalgamated. While
every care has been taken in the preparation of this guide, John
Bartholomew & Son Ltd. will not be responsible for any loss, damage
or inconvenience caused by inaccuracies.

CONTENTS

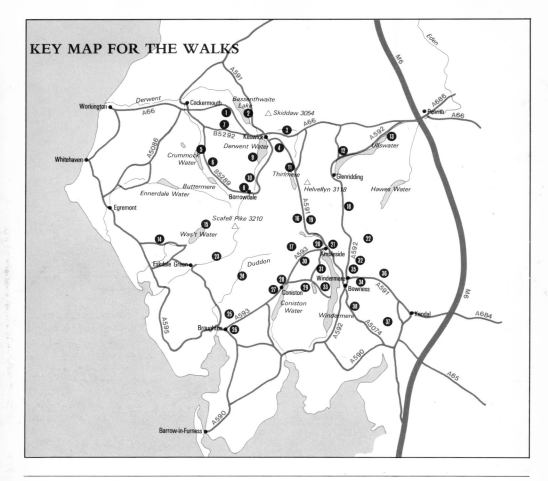

KEY MAP FOR THE WALKS

KEY TO SCALE AND MAP SYMBOLS

SCALE 1:63 360

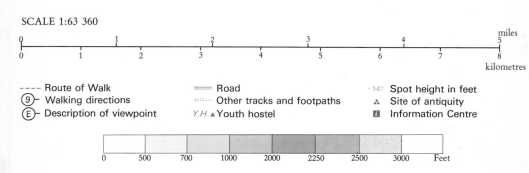

---- Route of Walk	Road
(9)- Walking directions	Other tracks and footpaths
(E)- Description of viewpoint	Y.H. ▲ Youth hostel

· 547	Spot height in feet
♣	Site of antiquity
𝒊	Information Centre

0   500   700   1000   2000   2250   2500   3000   Feet

1 ON THE REAL ART OF WALKING

Some walkers revel in mileage; some 'collect' long-distance footpaths like other people collect stamps while others run around many miles in wild country on map-reading races. Some would point to the need of modern spoon-fed society to tax sloppy muscles once in a while. But is there not also another, perhaps greater, need ? True recreation is a re-creation. In the natural beauty of the countryside one can find an oasis of reassurance in that confusing desert of changing modern values. It is a 'going-back' to the beginning. The true art of walking consists not of packing distance into moments, but packing enjoyable moments into distance.

Who would enjoy old wine by gulping draughts of it? It must be held on the palate and savoured slowly. Many perhaps could easily 'knock off' four of the walks described here in one day. That would be foolish when there is so much to savour in each one. What this book does, is point to a few features on these selected walks and leave the rest for discovery. What is left to the walker is his or her awareness.

It must be recognised however that in the normal human state awareness is dulled. Overwhelmed by the sensations pouring in at us from all side we habitually filter them out and accept only what we want and think we need. We receive only what we are 'tuned in' to receive. It could be as our own Lake District bard, William Wordsworth said:

'The world is too much with us; late and soon,
Getting and spending we lay waste our powers:
Little we see in Nature that is ours;
We have given our hearts away, ...' (1).
But all is not lost if we realise that these limitations are self-inflicted. All we have to do is to awaken our senses and willingly accept nature's messages in sight, scent and sound. That means complete relaxation in freedom. There is no need to accept the tyranny of a distance walking programme; no need to look on the Lake District as some vast open air gymnasium. Distance and muscle straining are not the objective here. What we look for in these walks is not quantity, but quality.

'Ah', some might say, 'but the best views are from the mountain tops'. That is nonsense. The best views surely consist of the two extreme elements juxtaposed; the active and the passive. Mountains and lake, or the frozen violence of steep crags set above the green calm of the dale. It is true that John Ruskin (1819-1900), the supreme arbiter of good taste in scenery, said 'Mountains are the beginning and the end of all natural scenery.' (2) He spent his last 25 years in contemplating them from the supreme low-level viewpoint of his Coniston lakeside house. A high viewpoint is not necessary; a low one is often just as good and indeed can be better.

The pleasures of these walks can be shared by any reasonably active family, which is why they were chosen. Beyond modest physical effort and a minimum of equipment, all that is needed is that 'eye to perceive, and a heart to enjoy'. (3).

References

(1) Wordsworth W. The World is Too Much With Us. *Miscellaneous Sonnets*. Part 1; XXX111.

(2) Ruskin J. *Modern Painters*. London, 1888. Vol IV; Part V: Chap 20.

(3) Wordsworth W. *Guide to the Lakes*. London 1835.

2 WHAT EQUIPMENT ?

For ordinary fell walking it is not necessary to purchase expensive equipment as though you were about to tackle the north face of the Eiger. It is bad logic to assume that, for instance, a pair of boots good enough for scaling the Alps must be good enough for Loughrigg Fell. Ice and snow are not the norm here. Footwear should be reasonably strong, not too heavy and preferably worn over wool socks or stockings. Nylon can give blisters. Soles of the boots should be cleated or wedged, rather than smooth. Sliding around wastes a lot of energy and can lead to falls and broken bones as easily as a fall of several feet. Boots should grip neatly and comfortably round the ankle so preventing the feet moving and rubbing into blisters. To summarise; boots should be strong, light, comfortable and provide grip.

Clothing too should be comfortable. As it can rain very hard in the Lake District it is advisable to carry a light rucksack with a light waterproof and if possible waterproof trousers too. These should protect you from the worst of the weather unless you are walking in the depths of winter, when more specialist clothing is likely to be necessary.

Carrying a rucksack leaves the hands and arms free. If walking as a family, the loads can be shared. It is always advisable to carry something to eat as walks can take longer than anticipated, especially if one lingers at a particularly pleasant viewpoint or quiet corner. A basic first aid kit with a few self-adhesive dressings for possible blisters and cuts, and an ointment for insect bites should be carried. In mid-summer it is a good idea to take along a proprietary brand of insect repellent.

A one inch to the mile (1:63360) map, as well as this guide book, is useful for putting the walk into context and for identifying the distant terrain.

3 PUBLIC RIGHTS OF WAY

There is more freedom to walk in the Lake District than possibly anywhere else in Britain. On offer there is everything, from easy walks by lake shores to rough scrambles on the high fells. The fells are open to all, not by right, but by traditional let. But it should be clear that though the Lake District is a National Park that does not mean that all the land belongs to the nation. Most of the land is privately owned, and farmed or grazed, and much of the valley land is enclosed. However, a vast network of public rights of way through this private land means that little is denied to the walker. With a map the rights of way can be identified; they are marked in red on the one inch (1:63360) map: public footpaths as red dots and bridleways as dashes.

The National Parks and Access to the Countryside Act 1949 tidied up the law on rights of way. Following the process of public consultation, maps were drawn by the County authorities of England and Wales showing all the rights of way. Copies of the definitive maps are available for public inspection. Once on the map the right of way becomes irrefutable.

What the right means

Any member of the public can pass freely on a public right of way, on foot, on a footpath, on horseback or cycle on a bridleway. No one can lawfully interfere with that right; not even the landowner. It would be wrong, for instance, for a landowner to move anyone away with the argument that the definitive map was wrongly drawn. It may be so, but until the error is lawfully corrected by the prescribed process the path remains a public thoroughfare.

The walker has the right to pass along the right of way and rest on it for a reasonable length of time. He has no right, for instance, to take a deck chair, a radio, and a picnic basket and sunbathe on it! The landowner or his tenant must not obstruct the right of passage in any way. He must maintain the stiles and gates on the path so as to offer unrestricted passage, a duty which seems rather unfair on him, though he can obtain help in meeting the maintenance cost from the National Park. The landowner must not erect any notice which might discourage, or lead the public to believe that a right of way does not exist.

A member of the public has the right to remove any obstruction which he might encounter on the route.

He has, however, no right to go purposely onto a right of way, knowing it to be obstructed, with the intention of removing the obstruction. It is required that any report of a known obstruction should be communicated to the Highways Authority (in the case of the Lake District to the Lake District Special Planning Board, Busher Walk, Kendal) who can compel the owner to remove the obstruction, or can remove it and charge the landowner with the cost of doing so.

A walker can take his dog with him on a public right of way so long as it is under close control. A farmer has the right to shoot a dog which is worrying, or he has reason to suspect is about to worry, sheep. Under the Wildlife and Countryside Act 1982 it is even an offence to have a dog not under close control in a field containing sheep; the dog owner can be fined heavily. Under the same Act a farmer can put a mature bull into a field crossed by a right of way so long as it is a beef bull, which is usually more docile; cows must be present too. How the ordinary walker can tell one bull breed from another is not clear. If it is a black and white Friesian, which is a dairy bull, it is illegal and definitely to be avoided!

No one can drive any vehicle, including a motorcycle, along a public footpath or bridleway unless he has the landowner's consent. It would be wrong to assume every motor cyclist on a public path is offending. Some shepherds now use motorcycles to get to, and to round up sheep.

The Highways Authority has the responsibility of maintaining rights of way, and the bridges on it, in reasonable condition. That does not mean, of course, that it should pave them all or do anything beyond ensuring that the users are not unduly impeded by extreme wear and tear. The Authority has the duty to place, with the consent of the Parish Councils concerned, footpath signs at the points where public rights of way leave public highways. However it could take many years, at the present rate of progress, before this duty is completed. The Authority can also waymark paths, and erect further sign posts on the route, if necessary.

The responsibilities
Rights usually carry responsibilities and these are a matter of reasonable commonsense. 'The rights of the individual should be thus far limited' said John Stuart Mill, 'that he must not be a nuisance to other people'. If a walker must pass through a closed gate on his route, naturally he should close it behind him. If there is a group of walkers, the rule should be not more than two abreast across paths on farm fields; every square yard (metre) of grass is vital to the hill farmer.

4 A CODE FOR COUNTRYGOERS

No countrygoer should ever drop litter. Everyone knows this but it bears repeating for the National Park authority, and The National Trust, using hard-pressed staff and volunteers, have to make constant costly efforts to remove the mess left by unthinking people. The fact that a footpath is clean does not mean, alas, that all walkers are respecting the countryside. It could mean that a group of volunteers has just cleaned it. It is no trouble to pocket litter until it can be disposed of correctly.

Obviously flowers and plants encountered on a walk should not be taken but left for others passing to enjoy. To use the excuse 'I have only taken a few' is futile. If everyone only took a few the country would be devastated. If young wild animals are encountered they should be left well alone. For instance, although they might not often be seen in full daylight, deer, both roe and red, are common in the Lake District. If a fawn or a deer calf is discovered lying still in the grass it would be wrong to assume that it has been abandoned. Mothers hide their offspring while they go away to graze and browse and return to them at feeding time. If the animals are touched it could mean that they will be abandoned as the human scent might deter the mother from returning to her offspring. Similarly with baby birds, who have not yet mastered flight; they may appear to have been abandoned but often are being watched by their parents who might be waiting for a walker to pass on before coming out to give flight lesson two!

What appear to be harmful snakes should not be killed because firstly the 'snake' could be a slow worm, which looks like a snake but is really a harmless legless lizard, and second, even if it were an adder (they are quite common) it will escape if given the opportunity. Adders are part of the pattern of nature and should not be persecuted. They rarely bite unless they are handled, a foolish act, which is not uncommon; or stood on, which is rare, as the snakes are usually basking in full view and are very quick to escape. Adder bites are rarely serious and panic is quite unnecessary.

For his or her own safety a walker should take care when walking on country roads. The advice usually given is to walk on the right so as to face oncoming traffic, but sometimes this can be dangerous. The rule should be qualified with the advice that the outside should be taken on blind bends so that traffic in both directions can see the walker.

Countrygoers should take care not to start fires. The danger time in the Lake District is usually in a dry spring when the previous year's bracken and undergrowth is tinder dry. A carelessly discarded cigarette end can cause thousands of pounds worth of damage.

Lastly, remote homes and communities depend on fell side becks and pools for their water supplies, even when the Water Authority's huge extraction plants are close at hand. Everyone should be quite sure before bathing that the tempting pools or becks are not someone's supply. Ask first!

When walking over enclosed land it is necessary to read your map accurately so as to avoid trespassing and damage to walls by crossing at the wrong place; a frequent cause for complaint. The stiles and gates provided should *always* be used.

5 MAP READING

A map is a representation, on flat paper, of the three-dimensional features of the earth. Some boast that given a one inch to the mile (1:63360) map of some strange country they can scan a part of it, and have a mental picture of the landscape it represents. This is possibly an exaggeration. The map certainly details the bones of the landscape; the flesh is left to the imagination. As a map has severe spatial and dimensional limitations it is necessary to interpret. This needs practice. Usually a family walking party has one good map reader and that task is left to him or her. This is unwise; everyone should have a turn! Map reading is important as it is the key to enjoying the countryside. Anyone who lacks this easily acquired skill is denied an essential freedom.

The map's key and the scale are detailed at its base. A brief study is necessary. Once the key features of roads, footpaths, watercourses and hills have been learned you should not get lost. One of the most common mistakes to make when map reading is the wrong identification of the point where you are standing. The path or road is identifiable but the precise place is not. The problem can be solved by correct orientation of the map; that is, place the map so that the top is towards the north. The easiest way to do this is to place a compass on it with the north point on the compass card pointing to the top. The map, compass card and the map reader (if he is to avoid reading it sideways or upside down) should all be turned until the compass needle points to magnetic north, which is currently eight degrees to the west of north (352 degrees on the scale). Once the map is orientated, some of the visible physical features can be identified and then with the aid of the map your position in relation to them fixed. Another way to orientate a map without a compass is to turn it until some identifiable feature in the landscape (*eg* a church) is lined up with the map, then all the other features should fit into place.

Orientation is particularly useful at a viewpoint when you are trying to identify distant features, such as hills or mountain peaks.

Excusably, one can regard the need to watch the time as a tyranny when walking for pleasure. However a watch is also a useful tool when map reading. For example, if you knew that it was 1100hrs when you were standing at the tarn and you know that your family walks about two miles (3km) per hour on a reasonably level route and that it is now 1130hrs, then on the one inch to the mile (1:63360) map you should fix yourself about an inch (2.5cm) from the tarn. This, of course assumes level ground. The other features on the map which one must master, are the contours. Experience might prove that you need to take account in your calculations of the need to add five minutes to every 100 feet (30.5m) of climbing, which is fairly average for a family. So if the journey from the tarn involved a 100 feet (30.5m) of climb as you see it from the interpretation of the contours and a glance back at the terrain, that takes five minutes (¹/₆ in/4mm) off your distance on the map.

With this formula you can estimate the time it will take to do one of the walks in this book, but to the walking time one has to add talking time, not to mention the looking, photographing, the eating, the sunbathing, and the luxurious idleness time. All this might be something of a challenge to map readers, but the exercise can be entertaining and the experience in the long run invaluable! However, good map reading still requires lots of practice.

6 SOME PRECAUTIONARY NOTES - SAFETY

The walks in this book have been chosen with safety as well as enjoyment in mind. However, accidents can happen even in the easiest terrain and 90 per cent of these can be avoided. There are the obvious precautions of keeping children away from quarry and rock faces, holes and unstable river banks. The falls which happen are usually caused by poor, particularly smooth-soled, footwear. What might be suitable for the town is a liability in the country. A fall can also be caused by the bad placing of feet, almost always *on the descent*. This usually happens when someone is in a hurry or is losing concentration from tiredness. Boisterous children must be restrained from running downhill. It is absolutely vital to look at where you are about to place your feet. Remember dry steep grass, or wet grass, can be as slippy as the other more obvious hazard of smooth wet rock. Tripping is another cause of falls. Watchfulness is again the answer. Accident records for walkers in the Lake District show a surprising number which have been caused by tripping over a dog lead!

Bogs in the vicinity of these walks are not generally considered to be a danger, but can cause some discomfort! Beware of ground which is bright green, or grey-green with sphagnum moss. If you find yourself bogged down, make for the bracken or heather, neither of which can grow on bog.

Even the most careful can sometimes sprain an ankle. Should an accident happen to a member of the family and you are near enough the road to help yourself, then you or someone else should try to get to a telephone. Dial 999 and ask for 'Police' and 'Mountain rescue'; give accurate details of location and, if possible, the injury. That is all that is necessary at that stage. If it is your practice to walk alone, then the most obvious precaution for you to take is to leave route details with someone at 'base'. This seems elementary, but there have been many occasions on which someone has not returned from a walk and no one else has any idea where that person intended to go. A search party has then to rely on guesswork; that could mean many expensive man-hours, or days before the casualty is found. If you leave the details, a search party has a better idea, at least, of where to look.

Lastly, safety of property; some of these walks start from quiet unobserved areas where thieves can be undisturbed. It is not a good idea to leave the car unlocked or valuables on display in it. Lock everything in the boot. Better still, carry no valuables at all.

7 GEOLOGY AND LANDSCAPE

The Lake District is basically a central mountain massif from which run a series of radiating valleys containing some 16 lakes. The landscape is of three fairly distinct types. In the north and north-west are the friable 'Skiddaw slates' which give the hills an angular profile. In the centre are the harder 'Borrowdale volcanics', giving the heavy, craggy appearance to the high fells from Gable in the west to High Street in the east. To the south are the softer 'Silurian slates' which give the gentler, wooded scenery typified around Windermere and Coniston Water.

8 HISTORY

In the 9th century when Irish and Manx Vikings cocked a snook at their sovereign Harold Finehair and tried to declare UDI, the prudent among them, probably numbering thousands, anticipating the wrath to come, decided to take to the long boats and settle in the Lake District. They flourished and gave the district many of its place names. Hills here are called 'fells' from the Norse 'fjäll'; the valleys 'dales' from 'dalr'; the small lakes 'tarns' (tjörn); the streams 'becks' (bekkr); and a waterfall is a 'force' (foss); rock outcrops are 'knots' (knútr). Place names commonly end in 'thwaite', e.g. Thornthwaite, Rosthwaite, Braithwaite, Satterthwaite from the Norse/Irish word for 'clearing' and there are so many other examples that Scandinavian visitors looking at maps and signposts can feel instantly at home.

The Vikings also brought sheep farming to the Lake District. Did they employ the native Celts as shepherds? That would explain the several old traditional versions of the way of counting sheep - from one to ten: 'Yan, tyan, tethera, methera, pimp, sethera, lethera, hovera, dovera, dick'.

The Vikings came very late on the scene however. The grinding glaciers wiped the slate clean of any signs of human habitation before the Ice Age, but evidence shows that major populations grew in the Neolithic and Bronze Ages from 4000 BC. The henges and stone circles date from this period and also the first major industry - archaeologists are still discovering how major - the making of stone axes. The 'factories' found so far are on the fells of Langdale and the Scafells where a vein of very hard volcanic 'tuff' (consolidated fine ash) outcrops; like flint, it fractures conchoidally when struck. It can be assumed from finds that the axes were roughed out on the fell and then transported to the sandy coast for finishing and then exporting. 'Langdale' axes have been found in other parts of Britain far afield, and on the continent.

In the Iron Age came the Romans with the successful northern campaign of Agricola in AD 79. To the east the Romans drove a road to Carlisle with forts near Kendal and Penrith; and later a road was made, no doubt following an ancient British way, from Kendal via Ambleside fort, 'Galava', to the fort and port of Ravenglass, 'Glannaventa'. The fort they built on Hardknott, 'Mediobogdum', ('The Middle of the Way') is the most spectacular monument to the Roman conquest and occupation anywhere in Britain. The fort, bath house and parade ground were built by troops who had marched all the way from what is now Yugoslavia. One can wonder at the sight of the ruin, perched impossibly on a shelf overlooking Eskdale. It stretches the imagination to the limits.

The Romans remained for four centuries. When Hadrian's Wall was abandoned at last, the tribal feuds, the control of which was probably one good reason for the wall's existence, broke out afresh and lasted for centuries. The border fluctuated and the northern half of the district was invariably part of Scotland.

The matter of fixing the border came by force of arms at last to William Rufus in 1092, but the Norman invasion did not succeed in taking control of the truculent border tribes of Celtic/Norse/Anglian extraction, who called themselves Scots or English as fancy (and hopes of gain) took them. The Norman castles took a good hammering before time at last took its toll; and although the Norman monasteries, particularly Furness Abbey (near what is now Barrow in Furness) had a great influence in the growth of local industries - sheep farming, woodland products and mining - they had to suffer costly raids. Robert the Bruce showed them little respect following his victory at Bannockburn.

The border raids remained troublesome until the 17th century and account for the scattering of defensive 'pele towers' where the local people with their breeding animal stock could take shelter when the alarms were raised. Cattle rustling was a way of life, romanticised in the old border ballads, but often bloody and cruel. The southern Lakelanders still have a saying 'Nowt good comes o'er t'Raise'. They refer to Dunmail Raise, the old border pass north of Grasmere. The northern Lakelanders perpetuate the tribal rivalry by repeating the same saying!

The border 'marches' were long subject to ancient agreed laws enforced, usually with great difficulty, by 'Wardens' on both sides. The notables on the English side included John of Gaunt, Warwick the Kingmaker, and Richard of Gloucester who made a home at Penrith Castle. One of the agreed laws was that reprisal raids for cattle stealing were not allowed, but thieves could be followed over the border in 'hot trod' to retrieve booty. To help in this hot pursuit, tracker hounds ('sleuth dogs') were used and good hounds changed hands at high prices. This may well be the origin of the still popular great border sport of hound trailing, where hounds follow and race along 'drag' scent of aniseed, laid down by runners.

The monasteries were very important local employers. They were responsible for organising marketing. Their dissolution was a great setback and adjustments were difficult. The thin acid soils and the exposed fells could only produce a farm crop of the hardy 'herdwick' sheep, a breed peculiar to the Lake District. The motto of Kendal is *Pannus mihi Panis,* 'Wool is my Bread', and so it was. 'Kendal Green' cloth was very well known as far back as the Middle Ages.

From the 16th century metal mining became a great source of local wealth. Keswick became a boom town. In 1565 German miners were brought into the town to help with their skills in prospecting and engineering. They established a colony on Derwent Isle. Some of the mines around Borrowdale and Newlands were particularly profitable, and copper and lead ore was brought to the town's furnaces in large quantities. Ore from the Coniston mines was also carted over. Vast amounts of charcoal were required for the furnaces and the forests were devastated. The northern woodlands never really recovered and only in the 19th century were conservation measures of coppicing and rotational cropping of the woodlands seriously used, although they had been practised in ancient times by the monks of Furness Abbey.

To the unpractised eye the dales generally show little evidence of human occupation before the 17th century. This is because until that time the commoners' houses were built of timber. But the older villages such as Hawkshead, and Troutbeck, and the older parts of Kendal and Penrith, with the wooden-framed buildings, are of special interest. Alas many of the old inns were altered to accommodate the tourist pressure of the last two centuries. However, the drystone walls are there to marvel at. Some of them date back many centuries, but most of them date from the Enclosure Acts of the 18th century. Some of the walls stretch for miles and seem to cross impossible slopes. The time and energy involved in their construction is astonishing. The stone was won from small quarries on every hill side. The builders lived and slept where they worked and were paid on footage. The advantage of drystone walls is that they can move as the earth moves beneath them, settling as they do so. This ensures their long life. The wall patterns are a major part of the Lake District scene.

From the 16th century onwards mills began to proliferate. Water power was plentiful and the process of 'fulling' woollen cloth was increasingly mechanised. The cloth, soaked in soft soap, was beaten by trip hammers. In the much later years of the Industrial Revolution the mills utilised the readily available coppice timber to turn bobbins for the cotton and woollen spinning mills of Lancashire and Yorkshire. One such bobbin mill is preserved as a working museum near Lakeside, Windermere.

Tourism came in the 18th century and it was in the early 19th century that it became fashionable to do the Lakes Tour. Poets, writers and artists discovered the Lake District. William Wordsworth, a native of the area in his childhood and schooldays (he was educated at Hawkshead Grammar School) settled with his sister, Dorothy, at Dove Cottage in Grasmere in 1799 and in nine years there wrote some of the finest poetry in the English language. His friend Coleridge took residence at Keswick with his brother-in-law Southey, who was later to become Poet Laureate. Other poets made their pilgrimages, and Sir Walter Scott visited Wordsworth's Grasmere home, taking his noggin at the Swan Hotel. Charles Lamb visited his friend Coleridge at Keswick and among other devotees were Keats, and Shelley, who took residence in Keswick for some months between 1811 and 1812. Later Thomas Carlyle and Lord Tennyson were staying guests of their friend James Spedding at Mirehouse by Bassenthwaite Lake. Then John Ruskin, a giant of his time and the supreme arbiter of good taste, set up home at Brantwood, Coniston in 1872 and lived there for the last 28 years of his life. The Lake District could not have had a better seal of approval.

9 THE NATIONAL PARK AND THE NATIONAL TRUST

The Lake District was already attracting great numbers of tourists before Wordsworth wrote his famous *Guide to the Lakes* in the first half of last century, and the wealthy were also buying tracts of prime scenic countryside on which to build their own country seats. Wordsworth in his Guide's concluding chapter expresses a hope that 'better taste should prevail' and adds: 'In this wish the author will be joined by persons of pure taste throughout the whole island, who, by their visits (often repeated) to the Lakes in the North of England, testify that they deem the district a sort of national property, in which every man has a right and interest who has an eye to perceive and a heart to enjoy'. Since that time there have been changes that Wordsworth would have deplored, but his 'wish' has received a good deal of sympathetic, if somewhat tardy, response. The world's first National Park was born at Yellowstone in the United States in 1872. The first practical moves in conservation in Britain came much later and took a rather different, perhaps typically British, shape.

The National Trust

Late in the 19th century the incumbent at Crosthwaite church in Keswick was one Canon Hardwicke Rawnsley, an extraordinarily energetic man; poet, traveller, athlete, historian, preacher and campaigner, as well as passionate lover of the Lake District. In 1890 a parishioner told him that he had been compelled to buy some land from his neighbour to prevent his felling some fine trees. Rawnsley accepted the idea that the purchase of property was the only sure way to preserve it, and he was concerned about the growing threats to unspoilt country and historical sites. With the supporting efforts of another great campaigner and reformer, Octavia Hill and another friend, Robert Hunter, Solicitor to the Post Office, an organisation was founded which sought to acquire and preserve property, by gift or purchase by public subscription. It was thus that The National Trust, a charity, was officially launched in 1895.

Some of the Trust's first acquisitions were in Rawnsley's own area. In 1902 Brandelhow, on the west side of Derwentwater, was bought by public subscription. Nearby Manesty Park was bought in 1908 before it could be parcelled up into building plots. Over the years since large areas of the Lake District have come into the care of The National Trust. Notable benefactors have included Dr George Trevelyan, the historian who gave properties in Langdale, and artist/author Beatrix Potter, who as a girl had met Canon Rawnsley. Thanks to her the Trust gained some 4000 acres (1620ha) and 14 farms. Now The National Trust is the largest landowner in the Lake District and has made it possible for traditional farming to continue in many dales, and vast areas of broadleaf woodlands to be protected.

The National Park

The Lake District National Park is the largest of the National Parks in England and Wales, with 880 square miles (2279sqkm). The Act which established National Parks came into being 140 years after Wordsworth's expressions of concern, and 77 years after Yellowstone. The first strongly organised pressure for National Parks and access to mountains came during the 1920s and '30s when walking and mountaineering became popular pastimes and access to open country in some parts of Britain was much restricted. The outbreak of war postponed progress, and following the reports of John Dower on the need, and the Hobhouse Committee's recommendations on implementation, an Act, The National Parks and Access to the Countryside Act 1949, was passed. 'People need the refreshment which is obtainable from the beauty and quietness of unspoilt country'. The provision for those needs of the people, and the protection from spoilation, were written into the Act.

In many countries of the world National Parks are areas of wilderness hardly influenced by man, and the land of these parks is owned by the nation or state. There is no true wilderness left in Britain. The 'natural' beauty of the landscape reflects the pattern of husbandry, and with so many owning and making a living from the land nationalisation of it was not contemplated. A British National Park is a defined area of unspoilt countryside, usually with some wild, if not wilderness, country, which is specially protected from unsuitable development; public access for its enjoyment is secured, and due regard made for the needs of the local community.

The National Park authority must exercise planning control, but must also provide information and ranger services. In the Lake District the authority also owns a visitor centre at Brockhole, Windermere, and has responsibility for the maintenance of public footpaths and bridleways. It also owns extensive areas of hill commonland, woodland and lake.

The National Trust, the charity, and the National Park, the local government authority, work closely with other large landowners, the Forestry Commission and the Water Authority, to provide protected public access unrivalled anywhere else in Britain. It is indeed as Wordsworth said 'a sort of national property' for those 'with eyes to perceive and hearts to enjoy'.

Addresses

The National Trust
National Trust Regional Office,
Rothay Holme, Rothay Road,
Ambleside, Cumbria LA22 OEJ

The Lake District National Park
The Lake District Special Planning Board,
Busher Walk, Kendal, Cumbria

Walk 1
SALE FELL
6 miles (9.6km) +900ft (274m) Strenuous

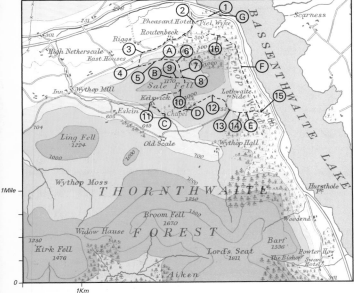

Sale Fell stands at the north-west of Bassenthwaite Lake. Its ascent offers no problems and is a glorious away-from-it-all expedition which is a great joy and highly recommended.

1 *Park in the loop of old road by the famous Pheasant Inn. This is signposted off the A66.*

2 *Go past the front of the Pheasant, then go round left onto the minor road and ascend it.*

3 *Approaching the brow of the hill take the green track starting through the gate on the left.*

4 *As a point is reached directly above the little church there is a junction. Go left on the green track.*

5 *Continue on, ignoring junction by quarry.*

A Viewpoint over the lower reaches of Bassenthwaite Lake.

6 *The track narrows to a path above the forest fringe.*

7 *An old ruined wall is reached. GO RIGHT WITH IT.*

8 *At highest point go right (pathless) to cairned summit.*

B Summit. The view, if there is clarity, is excellent. Northwards are the hills of Scotland, with Criffel (1,866ft; 569m) in Galloway the highest point. To the east is Skiddaw looking every inch a mountain from this prospect. Helvellyn is to the south-east and 12 miles (19.2 km) away. To the south is Grisedale Pike with Grasmoor and Whiteside to its right.

9 *Descend back to the wall by the ascent route.*

10 *Follow the wall down then pick up the green track on right making gentle descent by zig-zags to Kelsick Farm.*

11 *Follow the good track past the farm and on.*

C Ruined chapel. Once the valley of Wythop here had a substantial population. As it diminished the chapel was abandoned. It was replaced in the 19th century by the chapel passed by on ascending.

D Oak coppice. It can be seen that this fine oak wood was once well cared for and cropped, possibly at fifteen year intervals.

12 *After leaving the oak wood there is presently a gate right with track going down between derelict hawthorn hedges. Go down this past Lothwaite Side farmhouse.*

13 *Y-junction. Go left towards the forest.*

14 *Descend forest track to join clearer one below and go left.*

E Forest. The friable soil here can grow trees successfully. The predominant species here is Douglas Fir.

15 *Follow the good forest track and straight on.*

F Viewpoints through the trees to Bassenthwaite Lake.

16 *Descend to forest buildings. Go left through the group and on the track back to the minor road and round to the inn.*

G Iron Age fort. If there is energy left ascend knoll to mounds and ditches, the remains of the stronghold of a Celtic lord.

Walk 2
MIREHOUSE AND BASSENTHWAITE
3 miles (5km) Easy

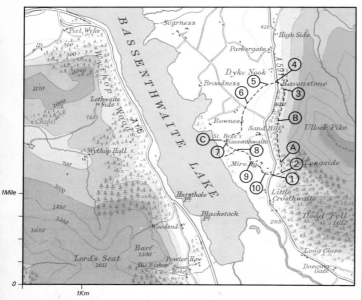

In the Forestry Commission's Dodd Wood forest south-east of Bassenthwaite Lake there are a number of walks starting from a car park at Mirehouse on the east side of the A591 4 miles (6.4km) from Keswick. However, this walk leaves the forest, taking in viewpoints and visiting the inspirational church of St Bega in its lovely setting by the lake shore. There is an optional detour to Mirehouse's lake shore and the point where Tennyson, who was one of a few great literary figures who visited Mirehouse, was inspired to write the climactic passages of 'Morte d'Arthur'. However, this is on private land used by an outdoor recreation centre for the disabled and, if this detour is made, a fee must be paid beforehand at the refreshment room in the car park. If you are here on a day when the house is open, a visit to it is strongly recommended.

1 *From the car park, walk beyond and round the refreshment room across the bridge and up the steps to the forest road.*

2 *Go left on the road, then right on rising forest track.*

A This is a very pleasing walk among some handsome Douglas Firs.

B Viewpoints over the lake as height is gained, the points depending upon tree growth and felling programmes. Blocks of conifers are usually condemned as dull, but here in the lake breeze the scent is fragrant.

3 *The track descends to road near the Ravenstone Hotel. Join road and walk (with care!) for a short distance to just beyond a cottage where steps descend left (signed).*

4 *Descend the steps and continue under pine trees and across left (beware bog) to kissing gate.*

5 *After the kissing gate continue on a causeway and on through gates to a lane.*

6 *Cross the lane and continue on a track through a kissing gate to the little church.*

C St Bega's. The church is probably on a pagan site. Why here so far from the road? Before the roads were built the lake was the highway. The worshippers would arrive by boat. St Bega was reckoned to be an Irish lady missionary who helped to convert Cumbria. The foundation of the present building is Norman. The setting for a place of worship is perfect.

7 *Leave the church by the way you came, but do not cross the stream. Go right with it to a track going towards the house.*

8 *This is the point where the option to go to the lake on the private path is to the right. (Go on to point 10 afterwards).*

9 *Short of the house a driveway goes right. This is the right of way. Follow it round past the courtyard.*

10 *Keep right of lodge house on grass track to road and start.*

Walk 3
GRETA GORGE
5 miles (8km) Moderate

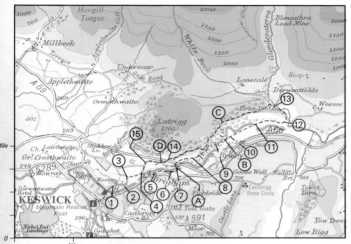

The approach to Keswick from the east must follow the River Greta which is fed by waters from Saddleback and Skiddaw and the northern end of Helvellyn. As the river flows below Skiddaw and Latrigg it goes through a deep gorge. Once upon a time the railway came this way from Penrith, one of the most scenic routes in Britain. The line was 'axed' and replaced with an 'improved' A66 trunk road which ploughed through the National Park against the advice of the Government's inspector following a public enquiry. This is a walk through the gorge among trees and by riverside and on part of the old railway track acquired by the National Park. The walk starts from Keswick centre, then to Fitz Park.

1 Cross the eastern part of Fitz Park (the formal gardens) and leave it at a gate in the north-eastern end.

2 This joins the road below the Keswick Hotel. Walk right, round the corner under the old railway bridge.

3 At this corner a track goes right. Follow this.

4 A path goes sharp right to a footbridge. Cross it to join the roadside. Turn left along the road.

5 Divert left to follow riverside path at the playing field.

6 Turn left down the minor road.

7 Cross the bridge then turn immediately right on path under the A66 bridge. (This path was made by owner's permission.).

A A66 bridge. Depending on how you feel, this bridge is either a marvel of modern engineering, or an intrusive monstrosity!

8 This delightful path through the woods divides. Turn right to the end of the railway bridge.

9 Climb up the bank to join the old railway track. Go left.

B 1864 railway track. It carried 240 000 passengers in 1882.

10 Cross the railway bridge and carry on along the track.

11 Cross another bridge and continue on along the track.

12 At this next bridge do not cross it (unless a further exploration is contemplated). The route is to the left to join a track. Go leftwards up the track to its top.

13 Junction. Go left to join surfaced unclassified road.

C There are views along this road of Helvellyn range, left, and the Borrowdale fells forward, left.

14 Cross the bridge over the A66 and continue on.

D Windy Brow. The stables and outbuildings here are used by the Calvert Trust which provides outdoor pursuits for the handicapped. William and Dorothy Wordsworth stayed at Windy Brow, the seat of the Calverts, for several weeks in 1794. William Calvert was a schoolfellow of Wordsworth's. Wordsworth became a close and constant friend of Raisley, a younger brother who died of consumption in 1795, leaving a legacy for the poet which gave him the independence he vitally needed during his most creative years.

15 Just after Windy Brow a lane goes left from the road. Take this and continue on to Keswick town centre.

Walk 4
CASTLE HEAD AND CASTLERIGG STONE CIRCLE
6½ miles (10.5km) Strenuous

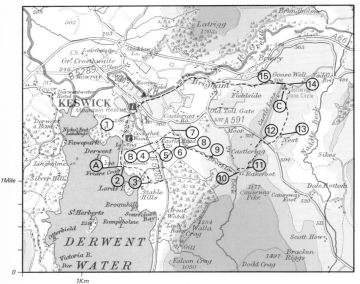

There are three places that must be visited when staying at Keswick - Friars' Crag and Castle Head for their superb classic views, and Castlerigg Stone Circle, a very atmospheric Neolithic/Bronze Age site as stirring in its way as Stonehenge. This walk should be memorable as it takes in all three attractions.

1 *From Keswick town centre go down Lake Road, past the boat landings and onto Friars' Crag.*

A Friars' Crag (NT). Here, so it is said, the friars of ancient time waited to receive blessings from St Herbert, the hermit who lived on St Herbert's Isle in Derwent Water to the south. St Herbert, tradition has it, was the friend and disciple of St Cuthbert of Holy Island. It is said

that in accordance with the prayer of St Herbert, they died on the same day so that they could go to heaven together. A memorial here records the words of John Ruskin that a visit to Friars' Crag was one of the earliest recollections of his childhood. The view, though from a low point, is superb, right up into the tree-clothed crags of the jaws of Borrowdale.

2 *Follow the path onwards by the lake shore and round the Ings property.*

3 *Follow the path left to join the roadside and go left alongside it.*

4 *Just after the speed restriction sign, go right across the road, up the steps, then keep right on the footpath.*

5 *After the quarry turn left, then pick up the path left to the rocky summit of Castle Head.*

B Castle Head (NT). This strange hump of volcanic lava is a puzzle. It is generally reckoned to be a 'plug' of an ancient volcanic vent which, because of its hardness, resisted destruction by the Ice Age glacier which carved out the Derwent Water basin. The panorama is remarkable and is explained by a diagram on the plinth. Derwent Water is below and the fells between Walla Crag, left, and Causey Pike, right, include the highest points in England.

6 *From the summit go down by the ascent route, but make for the lower right hand corner to pick up a path going north-east towards a housing estate.*

7 *Join the road by the houses and go right. Keep on, ignoring the left turning.*

8 *Cross the bridge by the farm and go up to the left between the barns.*

9 *Track elbow. Do not go left over the bridge, but go right to climb upwards with the fence.*

10 *Cross the bridge to the lane, go left along it for a short distance then right, over step stile, and on.*

11 *Path goes left at the elbow (signed).*

12 *Join the road. Here there is a choice. If there have been substantial amounts of rain and the traffic is quiet, one can go ahead up Castle Lane opposite and keep dry feet. However, be warned. The road is very narrow and if a vehicle is met the only escape is to squeeze into, or climb up, the hedge! The prettier, though maybe damper, way is described: Go right, then first left in a*

Over

few yards on a public right of way past the cottages (High Nest).

13 *After High Nest follow the wall and hedge to the wood side. At the end of the wood go over a step stile and straight on to a wall stile, then on, slightly left, to another 'fat man's agony' stile. Go on beyond, slightly left, to join the minor road.*

14 *Go left again into the field with the stone circle.*

C Castlerigg Stone Circle (NT). This was often referred to in the past as the 'Druids' Circle', but in fact it pre-dates the coming of the Celts with their druids by many centuries. It was built in the Neolithic period over 3000 years ago and one can only make guesses as to its purpose. It doubtless had religious significance but it was almost certainly also a 'calendar' to guide farmers on sowing time and harvest time. There are several theories on astronomical alignment, though some outlying stones have almost certainly been lost. Relationships have been suggested with the configuration of the outlying fells; Helvellyn is especially prominent to the south-east. But it is likely that in Neolithic times the area was well wooded and the views could have been obscured by trees. The entrance to the circle was on the north side, flanked by taller stones. The rectangular arrangement on the east side is unexplained but the Victorian suggestion that this was a place for human sacrifice is nonsense. The circle is in fact slightly oval, roughly 98ft (30m) by 108ft (33m). In all conditions the site stirs the imagination. In somewhat inclement weather Keats wrote:

'— A dismal cirque
Of Druid stones, upon a
    forlorn moor,
When the chill rain begins at
    shut of eve,
In dull November, and their
    chancel vault,
The Heaven itself, is blinded
    throughout night.'
(Hyperion II, 34-5).

15 *Rejoin the minor road and follow it left into Keswick.*

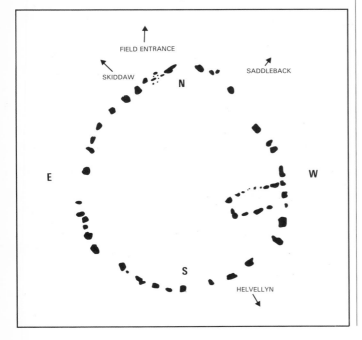

Walk 5
LANTHWAITE WOOD AND CRUMMOCK WATER
4 miles (6.5km) Easy

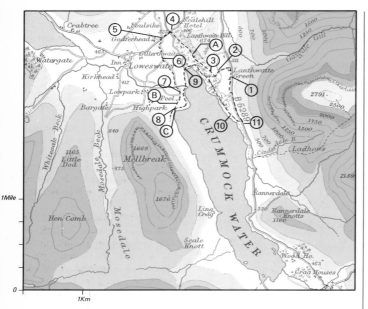

This is a very pleasant walk with a little climbing through woodland and by lake shore and with one of the finest views of Crummock Water. There are a few wet spots; otherwise the walk is easy with good paths. This is worth taking some time over, with a picnic lunch. The walk is especially recommended to photographers.

1 Park on one of the Lanthwaite Green lay-bys on the north-eastern end of Crummock Water, B2589 road (signs identify lay-bys). Walk north a little way and take the path just past *Lanthwaite Farm (signed).*

2 *Path bends right, then soon afterwards goes left alongside a wall.*

3 *Follow the pleasant green terraced track through the wood without deviation all the way.*

A Lanthwaite Wood. A beautiful mixed wood of 76 acres (31 ha) in the care of the National Trust, bought by public subscription in 1935.

4 *Join the road by the car park and go left over the bridge.*

5 *At the crossroads go left along a minor road.*

6 *Just after a house, where the road takes a right-hand bend go straight on, over a stile and along a green track between hedges. Then after a stile follow the single hedge.*

7 *The path comes within sight of the lake shore, but continue onwards. Go on to grass terrace path bearing right, past a ruin.*

B Pele. The name suggests that there was a defensive tower here and there seems to be little doubt. There are certainly signs of earthworks. The path has just passed over them. In the centuries of border disputes and raids this spot would be ideally placed for defence. In ancient times the lakes served as the highways and it is suggested that here stood a 12th century home of the Lindsays. There are traces of settlements in the Crummock area, too, predating the Norman Conquest by centuries.

8 *Continue on to shingle beach.*

C Crummock shore. A classic view over the lake in its setting of high fells. Haystacks is in the background, Great Gable behind.

9 *Go left to follow the lake shore by the concrete dam wall. Cross the footbridges then follow the path, keeping by the lake shore all the way. Wet places can be avoided with care.*

10 *Just after a ladder stile, left, the path crosses a little bridge. Take the path upwards to the road which can be seen.*

11 *Go left back to the start, using verges on both sides of road.*

Walk 6
RANNERDALE
4½ miles (7.2km) Strenuous

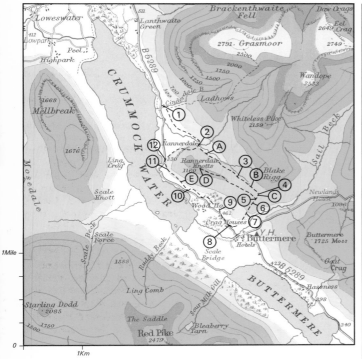

This is a fairly testing walk with some climbing. The rewards are a sense of remoteness and some excellent views. For the energetic there is the option of ascending Rannerdale Knotts (1160ft (354m) high), but this should only be done in good weather by well-shod walkers and the only means of descent is by the route ascended. Those who reject the option will still enjoy high level views.

1 *Park on one of the two car parks on Cinderdale Common on the east side of Crummock Water. Walk a few yards to cross the beck by the roadside, follow the wall up to the left and join a green track which goes right, climbing gradually.*

2 *Cross the footbridge and stile and go on path up the dale.*

A Rannerdale. There are mysterious tracks, ruined walls and dykes in this valley. There is the suggestion of a defensive enclosure. Nicholas Size, a local author earlier this century, suggested that here was fought a battle between the resident Vikings and the Norman invaders who were confused by the tracks which had been deliberately made as a trap.

3 *Wet areas can be avoided by detours left.*

B Dale head. Look back for views of Crummock Water and Loweswater.

4 *At the head of the pass turn right.*

C The Hause (head of pass). Fine view over Buttermere.

5 *Here is the optional path up right along the ridge to Rannerdale Knotts. Care needed! Return is by the same route.*

D Rannerdale Knotts. There are several little summits (knotts). A noble prospect over Buttermere. Great Gable is seen beyond, right.

6 *Several paths descend. Take the easiest route and go slowly.*

7 *Follow the wall side path down to cottages at Buttermere.*

8 *Join the road and go right.*

9 *Take the loop of the old road to the right.*

10 *Pick up the track (the old road) terraced on the right.*

E Rannerdale terrace. Another good viewpoint over Crummock Water.

11 *Rocky steps and steep descent to road. Take slowly.*

12 *The shortest way to the start is by the roadside, but if the traffic is busy this can be unpleasant. An alternative, if longer, is to divert right here to follow a path round to the footbridge and the fellside track of outward journey.*

Walk 7
WHINLATTER TOP
2½ miles (4km) +670ft (204m) Strenuous

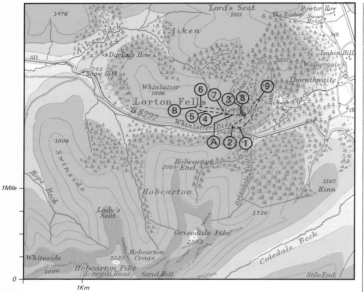

On the Whinlatter Pass section of Thornthwaite Forest, 2 miles above Braithwaite, the Forestry Commission have opened a visitor centre. A map of the forest is sold there and with it come a number of suggestions for walks from the forest. Most of them are fell walks and the Commission advises walkers to wear heavy footwear. This is understandable as the forest is very much a fell forest and all the tracks lead upwards! This walk to Whinlatter Top is not one of the suggestions and although some stiff slopes are encountered (smooth soles treacherous) one could hardly describe it as

a fell walk. First do go into the visitor centre where there is a welcome, and displays explaining the Commission's aims. Books and refreshments are on sale.

1 *From the visitor centre car park, walk westwards along the road to the next forest track entrance.*

2 *Walk up the track to the first junction.*

3 *Go left on pleasant airy gently rising track.*

A Quarry. This reveals the rock on which the forest is planted. It is Skiddaw slate, the oldest rock in the Lake District, formed from mud deposits laid down under a sea some

500 million years ago. It is possible to see here how the bedding plane has been bent by earth movement, near vertical at the quarry face and sloping towards horizontal further back. The slate is friable and gives a reasonable depth of soil for growing trees.

4 *Walk forward to the fence and go up it for a short distance. There is no stile but the low fence can be stepped over with care so as not to damage it. (It is to keep sheep out!) Walk upwards with the fence to near the top of its climb.*

5 *Go left on a vague path, then walk on over the higher humps of land to avoid the wet hollows. Make for the highest point.*

B Whinlatter Top. The heathery summit is a very happy place to be, particularly on a warm and lazy day. The view south is commanding. Hobcarton is opposite, as is Grisedale Pike. Causey Pike pokes its head over Outerside to the south-east. Northwards it is sometimes possible to see beyond Solway Firth into Scotland.

6 *Walk back to the fence by any route avoiding wet ground.*

7 *Recross the fence and return to the forest junction.*

8 *There are two tracks going left; take the farther one.*

9 *At the next junction (marked with figure 1), go right and descend back to the visitor centre.*

Walk 8

SEATOLLER WALK

3 miles (4.8km) Easy after initial steepness

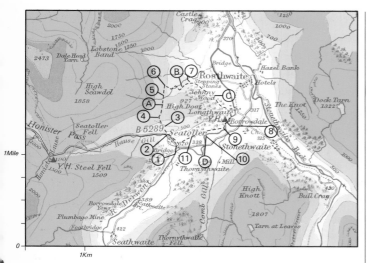

Good footwear is needed for this pleasant little walk from the car park at Seatoller, the hamlet at the head of Borrowdale at the foot of Honister Pass.

1 *From the car park, walk up Honister Pass past Dale Head Base, National Park Information Centre. Ignore the first path right which goes between stone gateway pillars. Go on up the road side to the first bend when a path will be seen going off sharply right up the bank and through a gate.*

2 *Go through the gate and ascend. Do not go through the gate soon approached, but go upwards left on the steep path.*

3 *Path junction. There are plain tracks right and left. The route takes neither. In between (forward left) a green path ascends to a gate in the wall. Take this.*

4 *A clear path is joined. Go right with the wall and continue.*

A The view forward is the impressive Castle Crag (Walk 10) and to its right across the valley is Grange Fell. Looking back up Borrowdale fells, Rosthwaite Fell is predominant on the left and the height of Glaramara is beyond.

5 *Cross the footbridge and go onward.*

6 *A broken wall is crossed; after this watch for a gate in the wall on the right. Go through this, go right with the wall for a short distance, then pick up the faint zig-zag path (green) which descends to a footbridge. Cross this and descend on the pleasant green path.*

B Scaleclose Force (waterfall). The ravine is so deep that the falls can be heard but not seen when the trees are in leaf.

7 *Optional detour to footbridge to view the gill. Afterwards follow the path on round the edge of Johnny Wood.*

C Johnny Wood (NT). The wood is a Site of Special Scientific Interest (SSSI) because of its uncommon mosses and liverworts. It is largely of oak and there is a lush undercover as can be seen. An interesting collection of trees can be seen on the left as the wood is entered. The trees (notably sycamore and an ash) were once pollarded. In the resulting hollowness high in the trees other tree species have taken root.

8 *The path goes along in front of the Youth Hostel.*

9 *Some rather tricky rock to negotiate by the river side!*

10 *There is an optional diversion to the stone footbridge which can be seen below left. This will interest those who like testing puzzles!*

D Folly Bridge. This was built from money donated by one John Braithwaite in 1781. Read the inscription on the stone. Queries: Why is this a folly? What has the fact that the donor was a single man got to do with the matter? Who is the father of the daughter?

11 *Follow the path on and it finishes at Seatoller Car Park.*

Walk 9
CAT BELLS
3½ miles (5.6km) 1100ft (335m) **Strenuous**

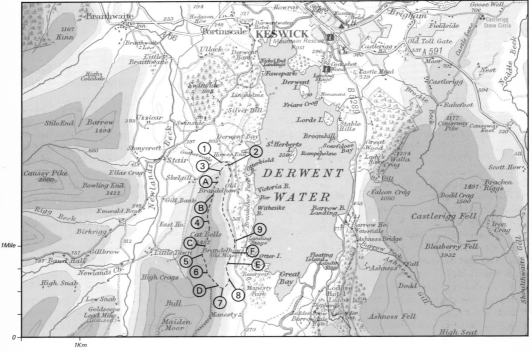

Walk the Lakes described a beautiful walk along Walla Crag on the eastern side of Derwent Water, with very spectacular views. Cat Bells on the opposite side of the lake offers the same stupendous prospects. The ascent is rougher and steeper than Walla Crag but it can be achieved by the average walkers, who, however, need to be a little nimble in negotiating the rock steps near the summit. Cat Bells has the reputation of being an ankle breaker or sprainer. Statistics show that almost all who become casualties were wearing smooth-soled footwear. Take heed. Well-cleated soles are necessary. This is a walk for a fine day when views are clear.

1 *The walk starts at Hawse End, the northernmost tip of Cat Bells. This can be reached by taking the service boat from Keswick landings to Hawse End pier, or motorists can drive to Hawse End from Portinscale, turning right down a narrow lane to a small car park at Gutherscale. Walk back to Hawse End.*

2 *Do not ascend directly from Hawse End. Go on round the corner to join a track going above the road. The path ascends from this track almost immediately. Follow the wide sweeps of the zig-zags. The longest way up is the easiest. Short cutters are ruining the fell sides!*

3 *The way along the ridge becomes clear.*

A The moment one begins to ascend the views start to open up. Derwent Water is seen in its entirety nearly all the time.

B The narrow ridge. Now Derwent Water and Bassenthwaite Lake are seen and below on the right is the Newlands Valley. This is a delightful on-top-of-the-world place to be. *Over*

22

4 *The rocky way to the summit is approached. Here again take the wide sweeps of the route. Some of the tricky steps cannot be avoided, but taking time to choose a route should present no difficulties.*

C The summit of Cat Bells. The views are extensive. Northwards is Skiddaw, its summit sitting back in the range's centre. To its right is Blencathra (Saddleback). Walla Crag is across the lake. Behind and right is the Helvellyn range, from Great Dodd on its northern end to Dollywaggon Pike at its southern. South-eastwards are the bulks of Ullscarf and High Raise and, surprisingly, the distinctive peak of Pike o'Stickle in Langdale. Southwards Glaramara is seen, but the high fells behind are obscured. South-west and very near is Dale Head. Hindscarth is to its right, and Robinson. Then right of that, way behind Buttermere, is Red Pike with Starling Dodd, its subsidiary peak, to its right. Then near at hand to the west are several arms of fell; from left to right their peaks are: Knott Rigg, Whiteless Pike, and on the same ridge Wandope then Sail and Eel Crag, then quite near with its distinct nobbly peak is Causey Pike, and to the right and back is Grisedale Pike. To the right again to the north-west is Thornthwaite Forest and Bassenthwaite Lake.

Little Town is directly below to the west. To those brought up on Beatrix Potter's books it will have a familiar ring, for Lucy lived there. On the fell side below was the little door of Mrs Tiggy Winkle's house.

It might seem hard to believe now but below in the Newlands Valley and eastwards down the fell side, there was a great deal of industrial activity. The Goldscope mine, south of Little Town, was worked from the 13th century, but in the 16th century it started in earnest. A mining company was formed in 1561, producing copper and lead to be smelted at six smelting works in Keswick, the largest operation in Britain and possibly in Europe. The company employed German miners who established a colony on Derwent Island, the northernmost island on Derwent Water. The mine was abandoned in 1864, because of the expense of pumping water out of it. South of the summit (and by the route of descent shortly to be made) was Yewthwaite mine, started in the 18th century. The waste heaps will be seen. The vein from there ran north-eastwards across Newlands Valley and ore was won by many excavations for centuries.

5 *Descend with care and join the path downwards towards the next fell, Maiden Moor.*

6 *At the hause (the lowest part of the dip) take the path descending steeply to the left.*

D A natural viewing platform is joined on the way down. Here there is a beautiful prospect over into the jaws of Borrowdale, with its woodlands and crags, Castle Crag being very distinctive.

7 *Quite well down this steep path watch for a path leaving leftwards. Take this descent.*

8 *A terraced track is reached, comfortably graded. Go with it.*

E Brackenburn. In the house below lived Sir Hugh Walpole (1884-1941). He was a popular novelist of his time. The most widely read books were probably *Mr Perrin and Mr Traill*, *The Cathedral* and *The Dark Forest*. He bought Brackenburn in 1924 and wrote the Lake District novels, *Rogue Herries* and *Judith Paris*.

F Brandelhow. Below here was a very successful mine and the spoil heaps, though largely covered by woodland, can still be seen. Brandelhow or Brandley mine was worked from ancient times into the 19th century. Flooding was always a problem. The final solution during the later part of the 19th century was steam engine pumps going night and day, though a thirty-foot water wheel was used to power the crushing mill. The ore was taken to Keswick by barge.

9 *The track comes down to the road. But it leaves again immediately, starting as a footpath and then becoming again the good track above the road and on to the start.*

Walk 10
CASTLE CRAG, BORROWDALE
2½ miles (4km) Strenuous

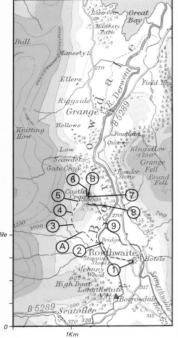

Many would insist that the finest area for natural beauty in the whole of the Lake District is in the jaws of Borrowdale. Its glory lies in its sheer jagged crags clothed richly with a great variety of broadleaved trees, breathtakingly beautiful in early spring and late autumn. Imagine this with a perfect high viewing platform right in the centre. It is there at Castle Crag. This natural

plinth was once the stronghold of a Celtic lord of Borrowdale. His fortress, ringed with mound and ditches on the summit of the cliffs, must have been impregnable. It yielded at last to the quarrymen, but even the scars of industry were quickly healed in this delectable spot, for trees have seeded and germinated freely. Thankfully the whole area is in the care of The National Trust.

The walk is short but the climb and descent are very steep. Vertigo sufferers might have some discomfort. Smooth-soled footwear would be deadly. The paths are rough and as always the best advice is to take a lot of time on the walk. Children should not be allowed to explore the quarries on the summit.

1 *The walk starts from Rosthwaite. There is a car park down a lane to the right as the hamlet is reached from the north. Walk on down this lane past the farm to the riverside and go right, along the bank to the bridge.*

2 *Cross the bridge, go through the left-hand gate, and up, inclining left to the stile in the wall gap visible above.*

A *Pause to get breath and enjoy the views over the valley behind.*

3 *The path inclines right to a gate by a wall corner.*

4 *Go through gate and upwards to join track. Turn right on it.*

5 *As the path descends a stone stile will*

be seen in a wall above with a path looping upwards beyond. This is the way.

6 *After the first part of the ascent go over stiles, then over a fence-crowned wall by stiles, go right to a grassy level, then left up the path through the quarry waste to summit.*

B Castle Crag. The mounds and ditches can only just be identified as the quarries exploiting the finest slate have bitten deep. The view is delightful and extensive. Northwards is Derwent Water backed by Skiddaw, with Blencathra right. Over to the east is the Helvellyn range. You may have to move about a little for the best views to the south-west, but there is no mistaking the Scafell Pikes range, with Great End first; the peak with the nob of cairn just visible is Scafell Pike, the highest point in England. Beyond is Scafell. Further to the right of this is Great Gable. But undoubtedly the scene stealers are the awesome tree-clad walls of Borrowdale itself.

7 *Descend carefully by the way you came, but only to the grassy level.*

8 *Cross the stile over the wall, then go left to descend the path which runs parallel with the wall through the trees to the river side.*

9 *Go along the river bank to bridge, and back into Rosthwaite.*

Walk 11
THIRLMERE SHORE AND GREAT HOW
5 miles (8km) Strenuous

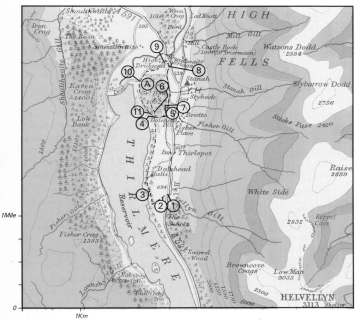

1 Park the car in the car park at Swirls on the east side of Thirlmere and the east side of the A591. Cross the road with care to the lay-by opposite.

2 Descend on the footpath leaving the lay-by, going by the side of a beck down to the lake shore.

3 Walk right, along the lake shore path.

4 The path eventually rises away from the lake shore and reaches a three-way junction.

5 Take the middle way for the ascent of Great How. (If it is desired to miss this, read from 7).

6 A path (signed) leaves the track for the steep ascent of Great How.

A Great How. A walkabout on the summit reveals several views. Thirlmere has a Scandinavian flavour from this prospect. Northwards Blencathra (Saddleback) looks every inch a mountain. Skiddaw is north-west. South-eastwards is the range of noble Helvellyn.

Retrace steps all the way back to the junction at 5.

7 Take the left-hand way around the edge of the wood.

8 Near a cottage the track joins the road. Go left on verge.

9 Take the minor road left.

10 Before reaching the dam wall, go over the stile left and along the terraced path overlooking the lake.

11 The path arrives at the junction again. Go right alongside the lake to the start.

The walk goes along the wooded shore of Thirlmere, climbs to a viewpoint hill, Great How, then goes on a woodland path and on an elevated lake side path. Thirlmere is a reservoir. The valley was 'drowned' in 1894, and the settlement and farms with it, when Manchester Corporation raised the level of the existing lake by 50ft (15m). At normal level the lake is now 158ft (48m) deep. The Corporation was much criticised for the large-scale planting of alien conifers. However the woodlands are now undeniably attractive and hardwoods are well represented. For years the Corporation's policy was to keep people off their property. Now all that is changed and the North West Water Authority, having put in a new treatment works, welcomes the public.

The strenuous part of the walk can be omitted if preferred by excluding the ascent of Great How, leaving the pleasant lake shore walks.

Walk 12
DOCKRAY AND AIRA FORCE
3½ miles (5.6km) Moderate

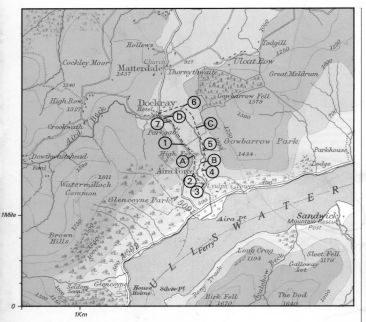

A Clay Memorial viewpoint. A very notable view over Ullswater from a little grass plateau. The land hereabouts was given to The National Trust in memory of Walter Cost Clay, a barrister and mountaineer who died in the Gran Paradiso mountains in Italy.

2 *Pick up the path below the viewpoint, going through a gate below a fenced plantation to pick up a path from a car park which is on the right. Do not go to the falls, but go down through the field towards the car park.*

3 *Double back on the path left to the falls. Go through the gate and across the bridge.*

4 *Climb steps, then go left on terraced path overlooking river.*

B Aira Force. Take advantage of viewpoints, particularly from the bridges. The longest fall is 80 feet (24.5m).

5 *Go upwards on the path to the right of the beck. When it reaches a ravine it zig-zags upwards to avoid it.*

C Alder grove. The round-leaved alder favours these wet areas. The charcoal produced from the wood was once much sought after and used in smelting iron. For making gunpowder it was considered superior to other charcoals.

6 *Go through the gate and go left in front of the cottage to a lane into Dockray.*

D Beckside picnic area.

7 *Turn left to walk on the verge down the road to the start.*

Aira Force, one of the best waterfalls in a beautifully wooded ravine, was included in a walk in *Walk the Lakes*. It is so worth seeing particularly after heavy rain, that it is included here with a variation. The car park at Aira Green can be full at busy times. This walk starts half a mile south of Dockray by an old quarry where there is ample room for parking.

The walk is set in Gowbarrow Park, once a deer park in the ownership of the Duke of Norfolk. Now almost all the land is in the care of The National Trust. However, the fields are grazed by sheep and **dogs must be kept under strict control.** During the critical lambing time when even sheep disturbance can cause losses, the farm tenant prefers dogs to be left in cars.

1 *The quarry car parking area is on the Matterdale road from Ullswater, half a mile south of Dockray. Park here and go through the kissing gate. Do not go down on the path to the river, but go right by the wall side.*

26

Walk 13
HEUGHSCAR HILL, ASKHAM FELL
4 miles (6.4km) Easy

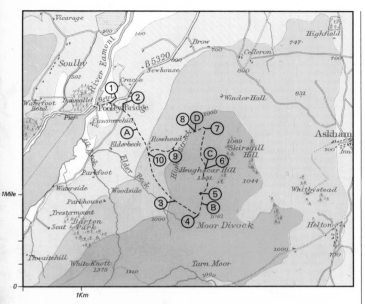

could almost grace a sports field. If it is fine and warm one is tempted to stretch out on it. White limestone outcrops enhance the plateau's charm. There is a view northwards to Penrith and to the east is Cross Fell on the Cumbrian Pennines. South-west is Ullswater and the range of Helvellyn, with Striding Edge in view if the light is right. Blencathra (Saddleback) is seen over to the west.

7 *From the north (Penrith) end of the scar an easy path descends to the track below. Turn left on this track.*

D Roman Road (High Street). The road follows the track left, but to the right the old route is obscured by boggy ground. It is thought that the road linked the fort at Brougham, south of Penrith, with the fort at Ambleside. The line it takes is remarkably straight along the fell ridges. Almost certainly this was a British road. The ancient ways often traversed the hill tops to avoid the bogs and watercourses obstructing the valleys.

8 *Cross tracks, incline right down towards Pooley Bridge.*

9 *At this point (by quarry holes) you should see a wall corner with trees beyond. The pony trekkers here have worn a track left. Our route goes down to the wall corner to follow the wall side down, then soon leaving the wall and descending left by a track to the track on which the route started.*

10 *Turn right and descend to Pooley Bridge.*

Heughscar Hill is a modest eminence to the south east of the foot of Ullswater and above the old Roman road of 'High Street'. It is a pleasant place to be and the views over Ullswater are unbeatable. The walk is a happy stroll, though there is some climbing.

1 *The walk starts at Pooley Bridge. From the village centre take the road out towards Penrith, but take the first turn right, by the church, for Howtown.*

2 *At the Howtown road junction climb on up the minor road opposite, and on to climb up the rough lane beyond.*

A Immediately height is gained the views open up over the lake.

3 *Cross tracks. Continue to climb straight on.*

4 *Cross tracks. A stone pillar here marks a parish boundary. A track leads left for Askham (signed), but left of this a path goes up the fell side past a broken boulder; take this.*

B A view is seen left over the Pennines into Yorkshire.

5 *Cross paths. The way is right, towards a grove of trees, but the path goes upwards to the hill top before reaching it.*

6 *The hill summit is reached. Walk onwards by the cliff edge.*

C Heughscar Hill. The springy turf

Walk 14
BLENGDALE
7½ miles (12km) Strenuous; some wetness

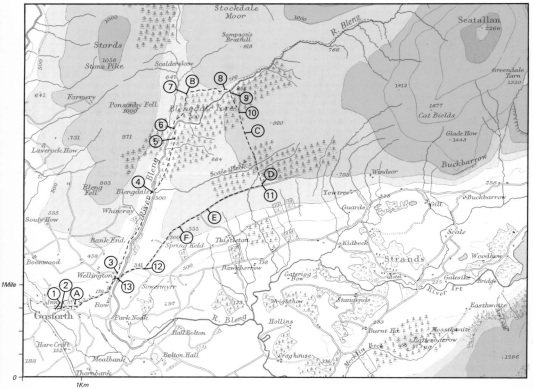

This walk is largely through Blengdale Forest, with a climb of about 350 feet (106m). There is one point which might cause worries for some: there is a stepping-stone river crossing. This walk should not be done after prolonged rain or the crossing might not be possible. However there is an 'escape route' if there are problems. Good footwear with well-cleated soles is necessary.

1 *The walk starts at the village of Gosforth, off the A595 in the extreme west of the National Park. Park in the car park and walk eastwards.*

2 *At the first junction turn left as if for Wasdale (signed).*

A Gosforth churchyard. This must be visited as it contains a unique slender Viking cross. When the Vikings came to settle in the Lake District in great numbers, most came from Ireland and the Isle of Man and there were converts to Christianity. Not quite converted? If the cross is examined it will be

seen that on one side of the shaft is the Christian account of the triumph of good over evil; while on the other side is a Viking version. Loki, the evil one, is bound, and Vidor is slaying the monster, Fenris Wolf. Walk through the churchyard and what is reckoned to be the northernmost specimen of a cork tree will be seen.

3 *Wellington. (The road to Wasdale goes over the bridge.) The walk route is straight on by the left bank of the river.* Over

4 *Blengdale Bridge. Go over it and beyond take the right-hand forest track.*

5 *Watch for a turning left, a track which is not as clear as the one which has been ascended. Take this leftward track. It descends, crosses a beck and then goes onward as a grassy track diving down to the river side.*

6 *Cross the footbridge. This is to the right and not easily seen as it is partly hidden by a bank. Having crossed the bridge, go left for a short distance then upwards on the track right, going straight on and ignoring junctions.*

7 *The track leaves the forest at a gate. Go right with the forest fence. Progress is not easy as there is little sign of a path and all is hummocky.*

B The fell to the left shows a great deal of evidence of Bronze Age occupation, with many burial cairns including a long barrow with the strange name of Sampson's Bratfull. Only keen archaeologists will benefit from a struggle up the hummocky hill side.

8 *There is a neck of forest and here the way turns down leftwards over boggy ground to the river side to stepping stones.*

9 *Cross the stepping stones.* **N.B. Take no risks.** *(If progress is not possible, abort the expedition here. Go back to the forest fence on the bank above the river. It is possible to step over the low fence without damaging it. Go then beyond the gravel pit to pick up the forest track beyond. This leads back down to the bridge at point 6.)*

10 *Continue up and on by the straight way ignoring junctions.*

C Open area. There is now a view across to the sea.

D Track junction. Looking forward, left, the Wastwater Screes are in view, but the lake is hidden by the hillside. Left, the near crag is Buckbarrow and way beyond to its right is Scafell, with the fierce face of Scafell Crag. To the left of this and farther back is Scafell Pike; the summit cairn can just be seen. Ahead is Muncaster Fell, with the sand dunes of Ravenglass gullery (nature reserve) at the edge of the estuary of the rivers Irt, Mite, and Esk.

11 *Go right on to the track between walls.*

E Viewpoint out to sea. The Isle of Man can usually be seen forward, right.

F The walls hereabouts are largely locked together by layers of turf between the stone. This is because the granite rocks here do not lend themselves easily to the normal 'jigsaw' building of slate common to the Lake District. Note how the turfs have been colonised by bilberry in many places, but there is a great variety of wild plants. Further down, hedges have been planted on the walls which could well be over three centuries old. These byways were almost certainly 'drove' routes, where in times long past cattle were driven to market, sometimes for long distances.

12 *Join the road and descend right.*

13 *Wellington Bridge. Cross it and go left into Gosforth.*

Walk 15
WASDALE HEAD
3 miles (4.8km) Easy

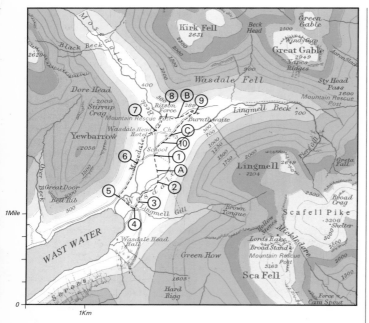

4 *A track T-junction is reached. Go right.*

5 *Cross the bridge, join the minor road and go right along it.*

6 *At the road bend go straight on over stile and by the beck.*

7 *A picturesque old slender arched bridge is reached. There is an optional diversion here to see the waterfalls. If this was wanted, go left up the path between walls and follow the beck up. Otherwise, or afterwards, cross the bridge and go left.*

8 *Path junction. Go right on the path following the little beck which it crosses and recrosses by small bridges.*

B Great Gable has dominated the view at the head of the valley, with Kirk Fell on its left. This is the best place to see the craggy face of Gable, very popular with rock climbers since last century. Styhead Pass, the way to Borrowdale, is to the right.

9 *Burnthwaite Farm. Go right, through the gate, by the farmhouse and right, down the track beyond.*

C Wasdale Church. This tiny dales church is a delight. Tradition has it that the rafters were made from the timbers of a wrecked Spanish Armada ship. This may be unlikely but ship's timbers they might be, salvaged from a breaker's yard on the coast. A tiny stained glass pane in one of the windows 'I will lift up mine eyes to the hills' is much photographed. In the churchyard are graves and memorials to climbers who died on the hills.

10 *Follow the track on to start.*

Wasdale Head is a tiny hamlet set in the most ferocious landscape in England. This is a level stroll there and the only hazard could be too much water. The walk crosses several fords which should be shallow. After rain one might need wellingtons. In flood conditions, which are by no means rare in Wasdale, the southern half of the walk should be left undone and you should start at point 6.

1 *Park on or by the green at Wasdale Head. Walk south to the acute bend in the road and go on the footpath in the corner signed to the camp site. Follow this clear path on.*

A Above left is the fierce face of Scafell Crag, with Pikes Crag to its left. The sport of rock climbing was pioneered on the 1,000 feet (305m) cliffs of Scafell. Its long climbs are still popular.

2 *A rather wide stony crossing is reached. Go towards the trees to the left, go over the stile by the gate into the camp site, and continue onwards on the clear track.*

3 *The track turns right into the camp site, but go on through the gateway on the left.*

Walk 16
HELM CRAG
4 miles (6.4km) +1100ft (335m) Strenuous; some wet areas

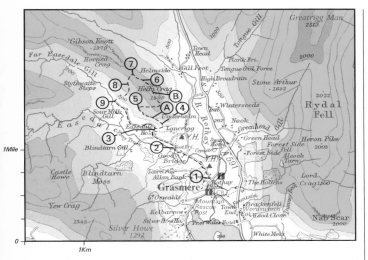

Helm Crag is the dominant fell overlooking Grasmere on the north-west. It is otherwise known as 'The Lion and the Lamb', for the shape of its craggy summit seen from many viewpoints. Until 1984 the public footpath up to the summit was horribly steep, eroded and nasty. But the owners of the crag, The National Trust, with the help of the Manpower Services Commission, engineered a completely new path on the southern side. This not only makes the ascent easier, but has presented the walker with fantastic views over Easedale and Grasmere. The walk still requires strong footwear and lungs to match, but brings it into the reach of family walkers with no great mountaineering ambitions. Although the top is

craggy, no rock climbing is involved in its conquest!

1 *Walk up the Easedale road from Grasmere village, past the Youth Hostel and on without deviation to the footbridge junction at the hill top.*

2 *Go straight on through the gate and on the tarmac lane through the field. The lane curves right at the end.*

3 *Path junction just past the last house. Go right (signed).*

4 *The path goes between walls, goes right at the end for a way, then curves left to climb the fell side.*

A Natural viewing platforms. The first one gives a view over Easedale, Silver How to the south-east, and from it right the long ridge of Blea Rigg on Langdale's flank. On the second viewpoint there is a view left over Grasmere lake with Loughrigg

prominent.

5 *The path is quite clear as it sweeps around the crags, steep in places. It eventually reaches the summit's south end.*

B Helm Crag summit. Here is a confusing mass of crags. The Lion and the Lamb is the first complex to be reached - but unrecognisable. The view is extensive. It includes part of Windermere's and Grasmere's lakes, and Esthwaite Water. Silver How stands over Grasmere, then beyond to right is a portion of the Coniston Old Man range. Crinkle Crags is seen behind Blea Rigg to the south-west, then there is Harrison Stickle of the Langdale Pikes and Pavey Ark. To the north in the distance is Blencathra, and then to its right across the north-west is the Helvellyn range, with the Fairfield range to the right of that and nearer.

6 *Walk on from the summit towards the ridge of Gibson Knott.*

7 *At the far end of the deep dip before the ridge there is a path going left down the fell side. This may not be too clear if the bracken is high and there are wet sections, but continue the descent here until a wall is reached.*

8 *Go left with the wall and then right, round its corner towards the valley path below. The worst of a wet section can be avoided by going right by a crag side, then left to follow the beck down.*

9 *All is now plain sailing. Follow the path down to the start.*

Walk 17
LINGMOOR FELL AND GREAT LANGDALE
6½ miles (10.4km) and 1,350ft (411m) Strenuous

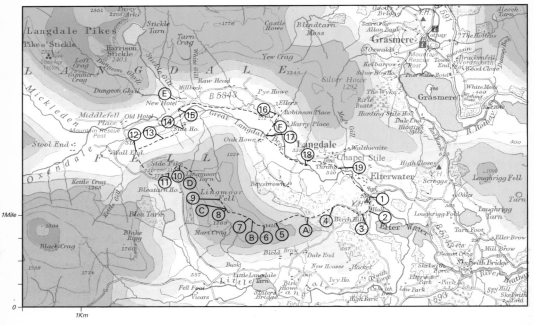

Lingmoor - the word summons up an image of open heathery upland and that is what it is, and more. Lingmoor is not high - little more than half the height of Scafell Pike - but it is its situation that gives it superb viewpoints. It is a dividing ridge between Great and Little Langdale, offering an airy view of the most handsome mountain valley on the one hand and Wrynose Pass under the great hulk of Wetherlam on the other. It also offers the best view of Blea Tarn, a view described by Wordsworth in *The Excursion*:

'Behold! Beneath our feet a little lowly vale,
A lowly vale, and yet lifted high

Among the mountains -
A liquid pool that glittered in the sun,
And one bare dwelling; one abode no more...'

This is an easy fell walk with some steepness and a longish valley walk to finish. Taking time to enjoy it, it might take most of a day. Strong well-cleated footwear is essential and the walk should not be attempted if there is a bad weather forecast.

1 *Start at the bridge in Elterwater village. Go south past the Youth Hostel.*

2 *Turn first right up the macadam lane.*

3 *Turn right again up macadam lane.*

4 *By a cottage the way forks. Go left*

up rough quarry road through the wood.

A Abandoned quarry. It can be seen from this platform that Langdale would have held a lake at the end of the glacial period. If debris had plugged the valley end, as it has done in some, there could be a lake today.

5 *After crossing a beck, and before a ruin is reached, watch for the path going upwards, left, and zig-zagging.*

6 *Go over the stile and then right to follow the wall.*

B First viewpoint. Views open up all round as the way is climbed. Backwards there is Elterwater and Windermere. To the north Fairfield

Over

and Helvellyn. To the left Wetherlam, of the Coniston Old Man range, walls the back of Little Langdale, with Swirl How and Great Carrs to its right. Right again is Wrynose Pass.

7 *Path leaves wall for a time at quarry dump, then rejoins it at its end, then path climbs rather steeply.*

8 *Go over the stile to the summit cairn.*

C Lingmoor Fell Summit. The views are extensive. Farthest mountain to the north is Blencathra (Saddleback). The Helvellyn range is to the north-east, with the Fairfield range before it and part of the High Street range to the east. There are the big ones to the north-west. To the left of Langdale Pikes is Great Gable, Great End on the Scafell Pikes range, then nearer, Bowfell with Crinkle Crags and Pike o'Blisco before. To the south-west is the Coniston Old Man range. Larger sheets of water seen include Windermere, Esthwaite Water, and Coniston Water. Loughrigg Tarn can be seen and, to the south-east, Wise Een Tarn by Hawkshead.

9 *Follow the fence on (do not use it as a hand rail!) over little summits and descents, some of them tricky, which may mean undignified sit-descents for some walkers. Then go on by the wall side.*

D Blea Tarn View. This is singular and captivating. To quote on from Wordsworth's *Excursion* (the bard having come across the scene just as we have):

> 'Ah! what a sweet Recess,
>   thought I, is here!
> Instantly throwing down my
>   limbs at ease
> Upon a bed of heath; - full
>   many a spot
> Of hidden beauty have I
>   chanced to espy
> Among the mountains; never
>   one like this;
> So lonesome, and so perfectly
>   secure;
> Not melancholy - no, for it is
>   green,
> And bright, and fertile,
>   furnished in itself
> With the few needful things
>   that life requires.'

10 *The peak ahead is Side Pike. Do not go onwards over the fence towards it. Descend steeply with the fence. Take plenty of time for this, the trickiest part of the walk.*

11 *A road is ahead. Do not join it. Go with the path parallel with the road to a stone seat, then downwards.*

12 *Do not enter the little wood. Go right.*

13 *The path is a little obscure across the fields. Do not descend to the left. Walk on by ladder stiles.*

14 *After stile and bridges above Side House Farm, descend past the farm and on to the road.*

E Dungeon Ghyll New Hotel left. Café and toilets.

15 *Walk right, along the road for a short distance by the car parking area, then take the old roadway (now a track) between walls. Follow the track through.*

16 *Join the road for a few yards only, then go right through the wicket gates along the track.*

F Old slate fence. Here is a classic viewpoint for Langdale Pikes.

17 *Cross the footbridge and go left along the river bank.*

18 *Cross the bridge then continue right past the cottages and behind the school to the road and Langdales Hotel.*

19 *Cross the footbridge by the hotel and go left along the river bank back to Elterwater village.*

Reference
Wordsworth W. *The Excursion* 320-350

Walk 18
BROTHERS WATER, HARTSOP TO PATTERDALE
7½ miles (12km) Moderate

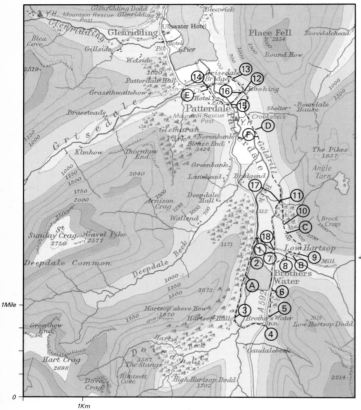

By comparison with the other walks in this book, this is reasonably level and, except after heavy rain, reasonably dry. Part of the route is walked both ways, but as this offers completely different views it does not detract from the enjoyment of a very pleasant walk. Strollers and photographers can spread it out for a good part of the day, carrying lunch as there are some good picnic spots. As the walk passes through sheep farms, **dogs must be kept under strict control.**

The walk starts at the foot of Kirkstone Pass on the Ullswater side, at an acute bend in the A592 just north of Brothers Water. Here is an AA box and a parking area.

1 *Cross the bridge and go left down the lane alongside Brothers Water.*

2 *It is possible to walk along the lake shore for some distance if preferred.*

A Brothers Water. The lake was once called 'Broad' or 'Broader' Water. Wordsworth remarked that the name may have been changed to Brothers Water following the drowning of two brothers, but tradition seemed to have it that two pairs of brothers were drowned there. The last two, according to the story gleaned by Wordsworth, were set to threshing corn on New Year's Day by their mother; instead, they decided to have a holiday and slide on the ice. They fell through.

3 *Hartsop Hall Farm. Go round behind the farm, and left across the field track.*

4 *Join the road by the inn and go left for a short distance.*

5 *A gate will be seen up the bank above the road, right. Go through this and left along the footpath.*

6 *Path finishes. Cross the road carefully and continue on the roadside to the gate on the left. A path then goes below the road by the lake shore. Take this.*

7 *When the path finishes, cross the road carefully onto the pavement and a path is seen right, going up between walls. Take this.*

8 *Cross the little footbridge into Hartsop village and go right.*

B Hartsop. Here are some typical 17th-century houses. Watch for a spinning gallery on a house on the right. It might seem hard to believe that this was once a mining village. During the last century and before there were two lead mines in the vicinity. The nearest, to the south-east, was sunk to 30 fathoms but there were several levels. Hartsop
Over

then must have been a very different place. James Clarke, who wrote *A Survey of the Lakes of Cumberland and Westmorland* in 1787, said of this valley's community: 'Vice and poverty sit pictured in almost every countenance, and the rustic fireside is no longer the abode of peace and contentment.......These fellows, who are in general the most abandoned, wicked, and profligate part of mankind no sooner settled here than they immediately began to propagate their vices among the innocent unsuspecting inhabitants. The farmer listened greedily to stories of places he had never seen......his daughters, allured by promises, were seduced; even those who withstood promises, and were actually married, were, upon the stopping of the mines, deserted by their faithless husbands and left to all the horrors of poverty and shame.'

9 *Just after a fork in the road a path goes off to the left (signed). Take this. It goes up a concrete ramp at the start and continues as a track.*

C Viewpoint. This is the best view of Brothers Water, yet seldom photographed. The track you are on is the old road down the valley. In the old days lead ore would be brought this way. Drovers also brought their black cattle over the track. The beasts were bought in Scotland, over-wintered and fattened in the Ullswater valley, then taken south over Kirkstone Pass to the markets.

10 *Three-way junction. Take the centre way. The track narrows to a footpath.*

11 *Angletarn Beck. Scramble left here to the footbridge, cross it and continue on the track. The way passes through a farm yard.*

D Crookabeck woodland. An idyllic woodland of mixed broadleaved trees.

12 *Junction. Continue straight on.*

13 *Side Farm. Go left here on the track towards Patterdale.*

14 *Join the road. The way lies left, but divert first right to the church.*

E Patterdale Church. Patterdale was probably 'St Patrick's Dale'. The church is dedicated to that saint, but whether he ever came and preached here, as tradition has it, is open to question. The present church is largely 19th century, by Salvin. Its pride is in the fine tapestries by Ann MacBeth, depicting 'The Good Shepherd' and the Nativity, with the local scenery as background.

15 *At the end of the village go left over the bridge and on.*

16 *Go right on track and along it; it is the track by which you came. Go straight on.*

F Viewpoints. The summit of Helvellyn is hidden by St Sunday Crag. The valley opposite is Deepdale, a typical glaciated valley. All the north-eastern-facing valleys in these fells are deep, rough and craggy, as they receive limited sunshine and the Ice Age glaciers with a slower melt would have lingered long.

17 *This time, at the footbridge continue on through the gate and along the track.*

18 *Join the road and continue on foot way to starting point.*

Walk 19
ALCOCK TARN
3¼ miles (5.6km) Strenuous

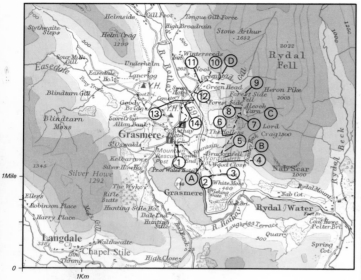

This is one of the most popular walks from Grasmere. The way up and down is steep but with care can be accomplished by all. The tarn itself might be a disappointment but the views are excellent.

1 *Start the walk from Grasmere Church. Walk east past the sports field and across the main road, then up the minor road opposite past Dove Cottage.*

A Dove Cottage. This was home to William and Dorothy Wordsworth from 1799 to 1808 during which time the bard wrote his best poetry. He brought his bride, Mary, here in 1802, later moving to Grasmere and then to Rydal when his family began to grow.

2 *At the road junction continue for a short distance onwards.*

3 *By the seat, take the stony track left.*

4 *The track goes between walls and divides. Go left through the gate (NT) and onwards.*

B Seat. View over Grasmere. More views are to come but this gives a good panorama of the village. After a visit here in 1769 the poet Thomas Gray painted Grasmere's picture in oft-quoted lines: 'Not a single red tile, no gentleman's flaming house, or garden walls, break in upon the repose of this little unsuspected paradise; but all is peace, rusticity, and happy poverty, in its neatest,

most becoming attire.' Not so much poverty, if it ever was happy, now. But except when the sports field is covered with tents or caravans, it is still neat enough.

5 *Continue upwards on nicely graded zig-zags.*

6 *The path becomes a rocky path and crosses an arched bridge.*

7 *Go through the wall gap to the tarn.*

C Alcock Tarn. To the right of the tarn are the best views. Windermere is to the south-east and beyond is Morecambe Bay. To the south-west is the Coniston Old Man range. At the head of Langdale, Crinkle Crags are left, then Bowfell and the Pikes.

8 *Go left by the tarn side to the stile, then on, scrambling left to avoid bog.*

9 *Follow zig-zags down with care. Do not attempt short cuts.*

D Greenhead Gill. Wordsworth enthusiasts will know this as the valley where Michael of the tragic poem lived. The odd construction over the gill is the aqueduct from Thirlmere Reservoir. A seat is a memorial to 'Tim' Oldfield whose efforts in the 1950s put many of the local rights of way on the map.

10 *Cross the footbridge, go left and down the track by the moss-sided beck.*

11 *Join the minor road and go left.*

12 *Swan Hotel. Go left along the roadside to Catholic church.*

13 *Cross the road with care and go down the path opposite.*

14 *At the bridge go left and then by riverside path to village.*

Walk 20
RYDAL AND LOUGHRIGG FELL SUMMIT
6 miles (9.6km) 1,000ft (305m) Strenuous

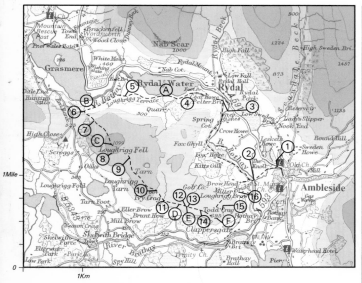

Although strictly speaking this is a fell walk, the fell is a modest one and most walkers would find the ascent undaunting. However, it is useless to attempt this walk in poor weather when all is obscured, for the views are all. If the 1100 ft (335m) summit is mist-bound it is easy to get lost and descend into the wrong village to enhance the taxi proprietors' incomes.

1 *The walk starts by Ambleside police station. On the north side go down Stoney Lane. Follow the path on at the end.*

2 *Miller Bridge. Cross it and go right along the minor road.*

3 *Before the bridge and main road go left along the lane.*

4 *Go down to the lake shore footpath and follow it west.*

A *Rydal Water. A modest little lake beloved of the Wordsworths.*

5 *Continue on the popular Loughrigg Terrace path.*

B *Viewpoint over Grasmere with Helm Crag and Dunmail behind.*

6 *At the end of the terrace go sharp left on a very steep path.*

7 *Stone steps lead to several cairned viewpoints which might make one think that the top is nigh. Summit is set back and bears a triangulation pillar.*

C *Summit. There are views over Windermere with Elterwater below and Esthwaite Water in the distance. Northwards there is a*

glimpse of Thirlmere. On a clear day almost all the high fells can be seen.

8 *From the summit follow the path south-east down ravine marked by stone cairns.*

9 *At a little tarn go straight on to the clearest green path.*

10 *Tricky rock step. Join the path below.*

11 *Go right of the little tarn. At path junction continue on, cross the beck to pick up path bearing slightly right by the wall bend. Path continues on with a wall on the right.*

D *Note some excellent examples of the drystone wall builders' art.*

12 *Gate. Shortly afterwards go through the wall gap and continue on by the green path.*

E *Excellent views open up over Windermere.*

13 *Path bisects a wall corner and by two gaps to avoid a bog.*

14 *Path descends through wall gateway. After it, descend no further. Go left to crag viewpoint. Ascend it from the left.*

F *Todd Crag. Viewpoint. The outline of the Roman fort is clearly seen. It was supplied from the lake and had a jetty.*

15 *Descend to tarn and then right on path to ladder stile and on.*

16 *Path goes through 'fat man's agony' stile and then down steps to lane. Descend lane to minor road. Go right for a short distance, over Miller Bridge and take any of the paths into Ambleside.*

Walk 21
STOCK GHYLL TO SWEDEN BRIDGES
5 miles (8km) Moderate

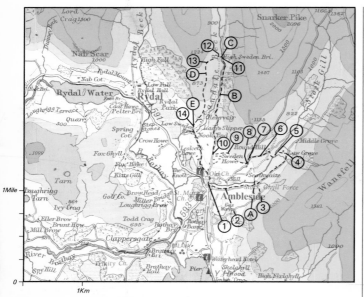

Waterfalls are at their best after prolonged rain. This could be called 'the waterfalls walk', but it makes a pleasant outing whatever the conditions. The three hours it could take can be stretched if a picnic is taken, and the fascination of fast running water can be enjoyed to the full.

1 *The walk starts from what was the market square and cross in Ambleside's centre. Between the Royal Yachtsman Hotel and Barclay's Bank is a narrow street. Go up this and go left at the top (signed 'To the waterfalls').*

2 *The ghyll can be seen on the left and presently there is a gate giving access to the bank. Walk along bankside path.*

A Stock Ghyll force. There are a number of viewpoints for the spectacular falls, protected by iron rails. The arched bridge affords one of the best. The ravine is rich in woodland vegetation where water has brought minerals to the surface.

3 *The ghyll-side path eventually leaves through an iron gate onto a road. Go left up this road and beyond on the track.*

4 *The track comes to a ford by the side of which is a narrow concrete footbridge. Cross this and immediately afterwards descend left to cross a bridge.*

5 *After the bridge, go left with the river bank for a short distance, then zigzag right to a kissing gate near the farm.*

6 *Go left along the lane to join the Kirkstone road.*

7 *Descend left for about 200 yards (180m).*

8 *Go right, through a gate and along a track between walls. Follow this track and path on through gates and stiles.*

9 *The path finishes by houses. Go directly onwards beyond on tarmac lane to the T-junction at the end.*

10 *Go right and upwards to join a fell track.*

B Rough Sides Wood. Here is a delightful piece of mixed woodland with the water falling below on the left. Here again the flora is rich and the woodland birds may well be giving voice.

11 *The track reaches High Sweden Bridge which must be crossed.*

C High Sweden Bridge. Here is a pleasant place to linger, by a traditional arched bridge and falling water.

12 *Follow a meandering path upwards with a wall to the right. Cross the stile, then go up to circumvent the stone sheep-fold. Go over the stile and join path descending leftwards.*

13 *Descend on a good path.*

D An excellent prospect over the head of the lake and Ambleside.

E Low Sweden Bridge. Another fine bridge and waterfalls to admire.

14 *Cross the bridge then descend right, back into Ambleside.*

KENTMERE HEAD
6 miles (9.6km) Easy

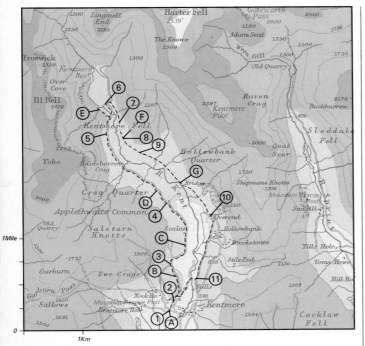

Kentmere has no through road, otherwise it would not be as quiet as it is. The approach road from Staveley on the Kendal to Windermere road, A591, is narrow and drivers need caution. The walk starts from the barn-like church at Kentmere village. Car parking is restricted here, especially on Sundays. The walk is by quarry tracks and through pastures and by quiet enclaves. A tarn, really a disused reservoir, is the goal.

A Kentmere church. The church has been renovated but there are Norman traces. Archaeologists are only beginning to discover how well populated Kentmere was from a thousand years ago. The long lake below the village was drained in 19th-century 'improvements'.

1 *Walk past the front of the church and up the lane beyond, left. Keep left at the junction and go past the farm.*

2 *At fork before building go left on green path between walls.*

B This is a place of many boulders left behind by the Ice Age glacier. But the many walls constitute a puzzle. Some were probably built to clear these important valley pastures.

3 *Join the minor road and go right.*

C Some awesome crags hereabouts, undermined by the Ice Age glacier.

4 *Hartrigg Farm. Bear left here. Road becomes rough track.*

D A view of the Kentmere horseshoe of hills is now seen. On the left is the High Street range. Mardale Ill Bell is at the head.

5 *Walk on past the quarry buildings and up a rougher path.*

E Kentmere Reservoir. A very pleasant place to rest awhile.

6 *To cross the river it is necessary to walk back alongside the spillway to the footbridge. Cross it then go back to walk along the dam bank above the oddly designed valve chamber. Pick up the path on the far bank.*

7 *Walk to the right of the quarry waste heaps.*

F Kentmere quarries (disused). The slate is of high quality, formed from sedimentary volcanic dust over 450 million years ago.

8 *Path becomes clearer.*

9 *Go through the gateway and round the ruin, to path beyond.*

G Arch bridge. Stop to admire this ancient traditional structure.

10 *Path goes by Overend Farm, then through gate to green path.*

11 *Watch for large split boulder in a field above on the right. Just before this a step stile in the wall leads to a path which goes by the boulder, across a footbridge and to a stile onto a path between walls behind. Go left on this. Follow the path all the way to the church and the start.*

Walk 23
BLEA TARN, ESKDALE
5½ miles (9km) +800ft (244m) Moderate

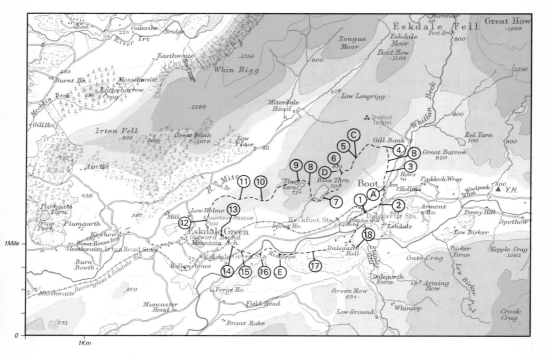

This is a wilderness walk for the most part in wild granite scenery, ending by a lovely riverside and woodland way. There is no guarantee of a return with dry feet, but for those with eyes to see this walk is an adventure. This is one of those elastic-time walks which could last for most of the day if preferred, as there is much to see.

The start of the walk is at the public car park at Dalegarth in Eskdale, by the terminus of the Ravenglass and Eskdale narrow gauge railway. If walkers prefer, they can leave their transport at Ravenglass and couple this walk

with a trip on the fascinating little railway. The journey takes about 45 minutes from Ravenglass. Allow about three and a half hours for the walk, longer for lingering, photography or sitting and communing with nature.

1 *From the car park walk up the road to the first junction.*

2 *Turn left through Boot village and straight on up the hill track beyond.*

A Boot Mill. The old Eskdale flour mill has been preserved as a working museum. It is known that a mill was operating in Eskdale from the 13th century, and it is reckoned that the discarded millstones here give

evidence spanning that length of time. The packhorse bridge is a good example of the type once common in the district.

3 *Y-junction in the track. Ascend left (signed).*

B As the way rises, there is little evidence to be seen now of the extensive iron workings at the far side of the valley. Forward right is the southern shoulder of Scafell.

4 *A group of ruins is reached. After the highest one, go left on the side of a hollow track and follow it on. In wet areas the way is obscure, but the track can be picked out with vigilance.*
Over

40

Remember that it follows roughly in a parallel direction to the valley below.

C Mine air shaft (fenced). This is connected with the mine at Boot, below. The mine was driven into the fell side following a vein running north-west. In the middle of the last century six levels were dug out, the lowest one being 660ft (201m) below this point. The mines produced a high quality haematite iron. The Boot mine and other mines in the immediate area promoted the building of the narrow-gauge railway which is now the valley's public transport. It is recorded that in 1876 the mines here produced a record quantity of 9135 tons of top quality ore, but by this time the market prices were falling and the mines were coming to the end of their economic viability.

The reason for the tracks here being hollow ways is that sleds were used rather than carts as transport. Peats were once dug on the fells here as a main source of fuel.

5 *After the fenced shaft the track becomes clearer, but do not be tempted off right on blind paths. The track rises and follows an old broken wall after a flat boggy area.*

6 *The way reaches a descent down a craggy ravine, but before taking it divert right to the top of the hill.*

D Bleatarn Hill. This is a delightful viewing platform on springy turf. A place to linger and admire.

7 *After descending ravine to the tarn side, walk on round the tarn's far side.*

8 *Continue on a green path. A little reed-covered tarn is passed left (easily missed), then a larger reedy tarn, Siney Tarn, is circumvented on the right.*

9 *The way on the far side of the tarn is not too clear because of soggy ground. The correct line is through a cleft in a crag and then across a little stream by a plank bridge. If you start to lose height into Miterdale you are way out of line! The path eventually, after skirting a bog, goes alongside a wall, left.*

10 *Go through a kissing gate then round a fence right to join a track by the wall of a forest.*

11 *The path follows the boundary wall right.*

12 *Follow the path bending leftwards to a ladder stile into the grounds of Eskdale Outward Bound School. At this point a path will be seen descending left; take this.*

13 *Cross the track and continue on through wet ground to a wall stile, and down to cross the railway line and on.*

14 *Go on through the yard to join the road.*

15 *Cross the road and go through the gate to the left of the fence opposite (signed). Cross the suspension bridge.*

16 *Follow the bridleway left by the riverside, then alongside a field to join a pleasant riverside path, then on into wood.*

E Bridleway. Is this on the old Roman road? There are traces of paving, and this is certainly the old road up the valley.

17 *Y-junction in the wood. The right of way bears right.*

18 *After Dalegarth Hall is seen over left, a track is reached. Go left on it to the road, then right along it to the start.*

Walk 24
SEATHWAITE TARN
4 miles (6.4km) Moderate

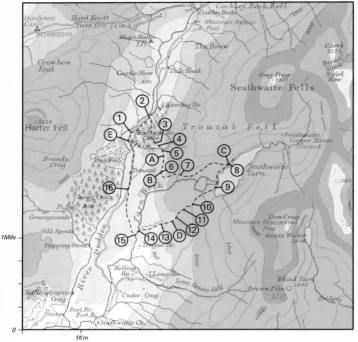

apparent.) Go right.

3 *The track becomes obscure; a path left can be seen; take this to follow a broken wall, then descend steeply to cross a beck, go through a boggy jungle for a short stretch and then go right to a wall.*

4 *At the wall leave the forest by a stile, then go left to climb steeply and circumvent the towering crags.*

5 *The path is obscure in wet areas. Approach the wall, then go right with it.*

A Valley view. The old farm at Birks is now almost surrounded by the forest which creeps up the eastern slopes of Harter Fell. When afforestation began in 1936 it aroused bitter controversy as it came at a time when preservation of the countryside and access to mountains was a major public issue for the first time and there was pressure on the Government to promote National Parks. Delayed by the intervening war, the *National Parks and Access to the Countryside Act* was not passed until 1949. As a result of the controversy here, the Forestry Commission agreed not to do any further planting among the central fells. In fact at this present stage few would say that the forest ruined the landscape. There was a further alarm, however, among conservationists when the Commission continued the planting southwards in 1983, but the planting was carefully planned in agreement with the National Park Authority. One happier feature of this forest is that broadleaved trees are in evidence to break up the monotonous ranks of dark firs. *Over*

This walk is across rough boulder-strewn ground with boggy stretches. Low shoes are not a good idea, as sections might be over ankle deep in water or bog, although the worst areas can be avoided with care. As the way is hampered by boulders, progress is not smooth and the walk might take longer than one might expect. So what has the walk to offer? Well, a walk into rather more remote country with those excellent valley views - down the Duddon - that connoisseurs of the Lake District, including Wordsworth himself, love so much. Duddon has everything that is best except a lake.

Apart from views, bogs and boulders there are some fantastic crag and rock sculptures carved and honed by Ice Age glaciers.

1 *Park in the Forestry Commission's car park at the head of the Duddon just north of Birks Bridge. From the Hard Knott and Wrynose road it is the first car park on the right as the forest is approached, two miles down valley. From the car park walk up the road northwards to the second entrance into the forest on the right.*

2 *The forest road joined runs more or less parallel to the public road, and in a short distance is crossed by a track. (The left-hand part is not obviously*

6 *Look for the gate in wall. Go through it. Two paths are in view. One goes straight up. Ignore it. The best and true way is right, on a grassy path which climbs more gradually and goes round the crags.*

B Look at these crags, particularly at those which have been scored by ice action. The rock is volcanic, of the Borrowdale series, the product of the intense and violent eruptions during the earth movements of the late Ordovician period 500 million years ago.

7 *The rather unlovely reservoir dam is in view. Keep left, close to the crags, to avoid bogs. As always in wet areas, the way is obscure.*

C Tarn side. In the sphagnum moss hereabouts can be found colonies of the sundew, a plant which gains its nitrogen supply by digesting small insects captured on sticky hairs on its red leaves. Close to the boulders can be found clumps of the mountain parsley fern, commoner on the hills of the Lake District than in any other part of Britain. Higher up the valley are the remains of old mine workings which were part of the extensive industry of Coniston Old Man, the steep western slopes of which can be seen across the tarn. There is little to be seen now at the mine sites apart from spoil heaps. Like the other mines of the Old Man on the eastern side of the mountain, it was copper ore veins which were exploited. Although such records that there are say little about the Seathwaite workings, they were fairly extensive. Eric Holland, the authority on Coniston mines, has suggested that, as there is no sign of a good track up this valley, it is probable that the ore was transported to Broughton by pack horses.

8 *Wander alongside the tarn if you have a mind to do so, but the way lies over the dam. Take this route to the track at the far side.*

9 *Walk down the Water Authority's road.*

10 *When the road curves left, look for a green path which leaves it to go through a gap. This is an old made and built up path, somewhat wet to begin with.*

11 *The path (possibly the old pony track) zig-zags prettily and follows a wall down.*

12 *Go through the gate by the sheep-fold.*

D Classic views down the Duddon valley. Black Combe (1976 ft; 602m) is in the far distance.

13 *Stile. Incline right to follow a wall down.*

14 *Stile and footbridge. Go straight ahead beyond, through wall gap into wood, and go left through trees and by a crag side.*

15 *Cross paths. Go right and follow through, bearing right near the end to join the road.*

16 *The road is followed back to the car park.*

E Birks Bridge. This cannot be passed without viewing the deep river pools below. In flood the volume of water is tremendous and occasionally has reached as high as the bridge parapet. The pools ('dubs') have been carved out into bowls by the action of grinding rocks swirling in the turbulent currents.

Walk 25
UPPER LICKLE
4 miles (6.5km) Moderate

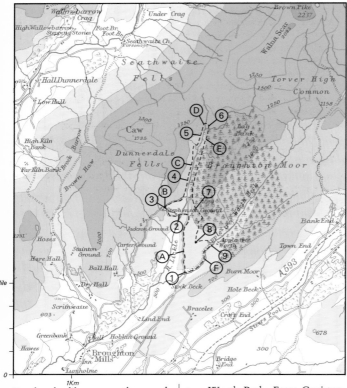

This area is the dividing line geologically between the Silurian slates, and the Borrowdale volcanics. The effect on the landscape can be seen forward, left. The Silurian soft rocks make for gentle slopes, seen in the foreground; the hard jagged volcanics make up the rather savage skyline beyond.

2 *Cross the bridge.*

3 *Stephenson Ground. Turn right just after the first building onto bridleway (signed).*

B Some puzzling ancient wall ruins here. To the left is a cylindrical stone-lined pit. This was a potash pit. In such places large quantities of bracken, cut around Michaelmas (late September), were burned to produce potash, used to wash fleeces. The raw wool was 'walked' in a potash solution, or beaten with wooden clubs. Or the potash would be sold to the 'fulling' mills of which there were a great many from the 16th century onwards. There was almost certainly one such mill at nearby Broughton Mills. Wool was the staple industry. The nearest market was at Hawkshead, set up by the monks of Furness Abbey.

4 *The green path is a beautiful terraced walk - how all fell tracks should be.*

C This is an ancient track. Look for old cart-wheel ridges in the rocky sections. A lot of the old ways like this, connecting valley with valley, have long been lost from neglect. Because modern means of transport are quick and easy, traffic is now concentrated on well made-up roads taking the longer, smoother, way
Over

People who like to see other people on their walk will not like this one. This is an away-from-it-all pleasing walk in a remote enclave of the Lake District. It starts at the entrance to the forest on Broughton Moor by Apple-tree Worth Beck. This is reached by taking the Coniston road from Broughton in Furness, after one mile taking the road left towards Broughton Mills, then taking the first road to the right (narrow with passing places) then left at the crossroads to just across the Apple-

tree Worth Beck. From Coniston, take the road to Torver (A593) and then on towards Broughton, taking the first road right after Torver, a steep one going towards Broughton Moor quarries. From this road it is again the first turning to the right to the bridge. If there is no room to park by the forest entrance, other parking places may be found by going further along the road.

1 *Having parked, walk on along the road.*

A A pleasant road through trees.

around. The old ways were spread about like the strings of a net. These important links were well made and maintained at a time when labour was plentiful and cheap.

There are signs that the valley of the Lickle was once well populated. During the 16th century the tenants of the large landowners (here William de Lancaster) were allowed to enclose their land. They became known as 'grounds'. In the Lickle valley there are number of such old grounds known by their tenants' names: in this case Stephenson, Jackson, Carter, Stainton and Hobkin.

5 *As the track gets higher it deteriorates into a hollow way with wet sections. A ravine becomes apparent on the right, crossed by a wooden footbridge. The way lies over this bridge, but to reach it the track must be followed to a higher level and it is necessary to double back, keeping high to avoid a large bog.*

D Ravine. Junipers cling precariously to the side. Look back for a view out to sea over the estuary.

6 *Cross the bridge, enter the forest, and go down the forest road.*

E The planting, as one descends, is Norway spruce to the left (Christmas trees) and Sitka spruce right. Lower down there are larch left and cypress right. A good view opens out to the south over the Duddon estuary to the sea.

7 *Nearing the bottom of the forest the track forks. Go left.*

8 *T-junction. Go left (apparently the wrong direction initially, but briefly.)*

9 *Junction by farm ruin - Apple-tree Worth. Go very sharply right.*

F As the starting point is approached, a land-slip (right) shows an interesting exposure of metamorphose rock: rock affected by the super heat of volcanic action.

Walk 26
LATTER RIGG AND WOODLAND
5½ miles (9km) Moderate

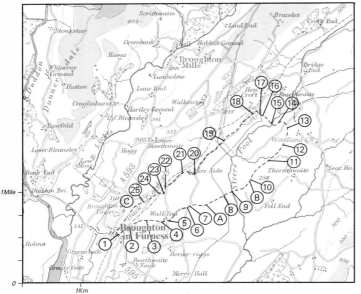

shortly, going right over a stone stair stile, then go left alongside the line, through a stile.

3 When approaching another wall, go right and through a narrow stile and continue on by the field boundary.

4 Go through another stile and then left on the track towards the farm.

5 Go by the farm, through a gate, go right on a tarmac lane then immediately left down a track through the wood, and on through a plantation.

6 Join a minor road, and go left by it up the hill.

7 In a short distance go right on the footpath (signed).

A Coniston Old Man from this viewpoint looks a compact mass. All the land between here and the mountain is in the Silurian slate area. It is much softer than the hard Borrowdale volcanics of the central fells of which the Old Man is part; hence it was flattened more easily by the thrusting action of the Ice Age glaciers.

8 The path crosses a bridge over a drainage ditch.

9 Cross the beck by the footbridge, after which follow the fence on the right, then at its end bear left to go through a fence gap to join a track going left under the hill side.

B After the Ice Age, what are now only scattered watercourses would have been one huge river. There is evidence that in Bronze Age times the slightly higher land to the east and west supported a sizeable population of farmers. One such settlement still identifiable by stone walls and hut circles is only two *Over*

As there is very little climbing in this walk, it should have been classed as 'easy', but a certain amount of agility is required to negotiate the rough stiles and gates. The route from Broughton in Furness is in the mild rolling countryside of the Silurian slates around a plain which, after the Ice Age and the floods which followed, must have been an estuary. This is a walk for naturalists in a quiet area.

Broughton is one of those unspoilt villages which is handsome rather than pretty. It is an ancient township with a market charter. It lost its strategic importance when Ulverston took trade following the making of the Ulverston Canal, which gave that market access to the sea. The tradition of reading out the charter on the first of August at the market cross is still maintained, after which bags of new pennies are scattered among the local children. In earlier, harsher times the pennies were first heated. The market square is the best feature of the little town. The old stone slabs of the market stalls are still there, and the stocks. An obelisk records the benevolence of John Gilpin who gave the land for the market. A plaque on the Market Hall wall states that the square was designed in 1766 by a 'London Architect' no less!

1 Leave the market square and walk downhill past the Mountain Centre shop then turn left by the road junction to go up what was obviously the old railway line, alas now gone.

2 Leave the old railway line route

miles to the south-east. Evidence of other populations is all around in the form of burial mounds. It can be imagined that the ancient herdsmen brought their animals here to take the early spring grass. For many centuries this land has provided grazing for animals; if it had not done so, it would be covered with scrub and trees. The climate here is much milder than that further inland. The land is comparatively rich in nutrients. The soil in the surrounding higher land is poor and acid. Here the surface layer of the soil is peaty and retains moisture, as you may discover!

10 *Stone step stile. After this the way is a little obscure for a time. Ignore the path right up the fell. Go onwards past the hawthorn tree and three silver birches, then go left slightly towards some mountain ash (rowan) trees and higher ground when a plainer path should be picked up.*

11 *Ignore the track leaving to go right upwards; the way lies forward towards a wall corner which should be seen.*

12 *Cross tracks. Go left on slight descent.*

13 *More cross tracks. Bear left.*

14 *The way becomes plainer as it follows the wall on the right.*

15 *Watch for a stile in the wall on the right and a path leading to a footbridge. Cross the bridge and follow the field boundary on the left.*

16 *Stile on left. At the time of writing this is obstructed by blackthorn, but this is no real problem as there are gaps in the old hedge alongside. Pass through and go right.*

17 *There should be a stile here into the wood. At the time of writing it was not there, but until the stile is replaced it is possible to squeeze through between the fence end and wall. Walk up to a track in the wood, and go left along it.*

18 *Follow the track straight on.*

19 *Join the minor road and go left along it.*

20 *Mireside Farm is by a bend in the road. Go up through the farmyard, through a gate, then right, along and up a track.*

21 *The old railway line is ahead, but just before it a green lane goes left through a gate. Take this. It goes between walls. Go through a gate as the walled section finishes, and follow the field boundary on the right, watching for a stile.*

22 *Go through the stile and incline right towards the field boundary by the railway line.*

23 *Go over stone stair stile onto old railway line. Beyond, go over the stair stile at the other side of the track.*

24 *Incline leftwards to the field corner and into parkland.*

25 *Follow the green track through the park, leftwards by the ha-ha (sunken fence) boundary of Broughton Hall, through an iron gate and on through the park to the village centre.*

C Broughton Tower. This is not open to the public. Part of it is a 14th-century 'pele' tower. Until the 15th century this was the seat of the Broughton family, then it was lost to them as a result of a political gamble. Sir Thomas Broughton supported the pretender Lambert Simnel, who landed with an army of mercenaries at Swarthmoor near Ulverston across the sands after being crowned King of England in Dublin in 1487. When Lambert Simnel was defeated at Stokefield Henry VII sought out the traitorous supporters. Tradition has it that Sir Thomas fled eastwards to hide in the Witherslack woods, where he was supported by faithful retainers. Broughton Tower was gifted by the king to the Stanleys.

Walk 27

WALNA SCAR AND CONISTON SHORE

7 miles (11km) Moderate

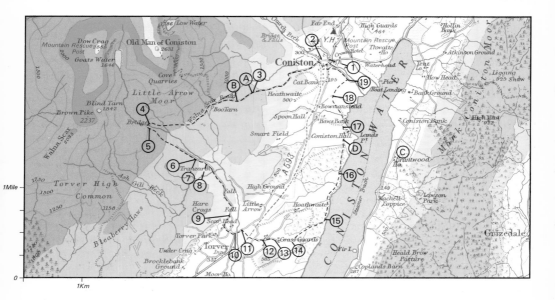

This walk takes the old road, now a rough track, between Coniston and Seathwaite in Dunnerdale, the Walna Scar, then descends by old quarries to Torver, and returns by the lake shore. Strong footwear is necessary for this and there may be unavoidable wet sections.

Walna Scar was once an important road linking the settlements in the Duddon valley with Coniston and Hawkshead. The monks of Furness Abbey established the wool market at Hawkshead so the link was vital in the Middle Ages to the main industry. The road very probably has greater antiquity as there are signs of Bronze Age settlements in the area. With other road improvements being made, Walna Scar was allowed to deteriorate. The

quarry vehicles are now the only regular users.

1 *From Coniston village centre walk south, cross the bridge, pass the garage, and then turn right, up the hill.*

2 *At the road junction incline left to climb the steep tarmac lane. Continue straight up it.*

3 *At the fell gate and cross tracks, go through the gate and straight on.*

A Fell gate. There is a view of Coniston Old Man, right.

B Bursting Stone Quarry is still active above. The slate, in the Borrowdale volcanic series, is extremely hard and takes an attractive polish. It is exported widely and now used largely for putting a decorative face on buildings. Coniston slates have been quarried for centuries but the

industry really took off in the great building time during the 17th and 18th centuries. The slates from the Coniston Old Man quarries were carried down to Kirkby Quay on the lake shore and barged down to Nibthwaite at the lake foot, then carried down by cart to the port at Greenodd, or at Ulverston. Most of the slate was hand-dressed by skilled workmen for roofing purposes. There are many abandoned quarries around the mountain.

4 *Cross the arched bridge.*

5 *Descend left. There are several paths: choose the dryest. Aim for the gateway in the wall below. Go through the gateway and straight on.*

6 *The path goes between two quarry holes.*

Over

7 *Go right of the quarry waste heap and descend between walls. Go through the gates by sheep pens and past the buildings (Tranearth).*

8 *Go straight down, cross the bridge and descend between walls.*

9 *At the junction keep right. Then descend by macadam lane to the road.*

10 *Turn left along the roadside and cross the bridge.*

11 *Immediately after the bridge, go right through the kissing gate to follow the fence and wall, turning right to go through 'fat man's agony' stile and on by other stiles over what was the old railway line. Go left of the ruin and through the stile by a gate onto a lane.*

12 *Cross the lane and go between fences and hedges opposite. The way turns between buildings and then deteriorates. Take right-hand gate and go on old lane between banks.*

13 *There is often wetness here. Avoid it as best you can. Pass a ruin and on, on obvious path. Follow this down through the gate and on.*

14 *There is a fork on the descent. Keep left down through the wood to the lake shore.*

C Brantwood is the white house across the lake. Here John Ruskin lived from 1871 until his death in 1900. First Slade Professor of Fine Art at Oxford, artist, author, philosopher, he was a giant of his time. Brantwood, which he extended considerably, was his retreat. He was a great champion for the preservation of the Lake District. Brantwood is open to the public and contains many of Ruskin's treasures. Other exhibits can be seen in Coniston Museum which is well worth a visit.

In places on the shore slag may be found. This originates from ancient 'bloomeries' where iron was smelted. The lake shore area was a favourite place for these crude furnaces. The ore was brought to the site from the Furness mines, by boat. The charcoal fuel was obtained from the extensive woodlands on the slopes above. Occasionally the woods were devastated by this activity. Probably the monks of Furness Abbey promoted this industry. The baron of Kendal allowed the monks to have one boat 'to carry what might be necessary upon the lake of Thurstainwater' (the old name for Coniston Water).

15 *Go on left along the lake shore path.*

16 *The path leaves the lake shore and heads for Coniston Hall, the old house with cylindrical chimneys.*

D Coniston Hall. The hall dates from the late 16th century. Cylindrical chimneys in the Lake District are typical in old buildings, the shape being easier to construct from undressed stone. From 1250 this site was the home of the Flemings who owned much of the area and eventually made great profit from the Coniston Old Man's copper mines. In the 18th century the family moved to Rydal Hall. The Wordsworths were their tenants when they lived at Rydal Mount. The hall was neglected but it has been restored in recent years by the owners, The National Trust.

17 *After the hall a lane bends left. Follow it for a short distance, then go right on a path across the fields parallel with the lake. Go through the gateway and over the bridge; take the path inclining left towards the village.*

18 *Just before the wood there is a path junction. Go right on elevated track.*

19 *The path joins a roadway; go left on it to the village.*

Walk 28
CONISTON COPPER MINES VALLEY AND LEVERS WATER
4 miles (6.4km) Strenuous

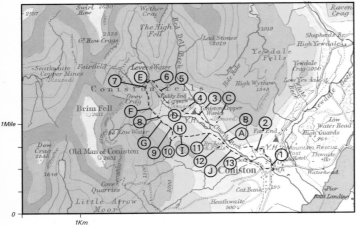

Coniston Old Man is riddled with old mines. The mineral wealth of the area was possibly exploited from Roman times, and most probably also by the monks of Furness Abbey. But before the 16th century work would have been confined to the area of the surface veins. By the 17th century, mining was done in earnest with the use of German immigrants. Work increased into the 19th century when mines had penetrated to a depth of over a thousand feet. Now the only signs of the great activity are vast waste heaps, and crumbling entrances and holes, and the old tracks. This walk goes up into Copper Mines Valley under the crags of the Old Man, past Levers Water, which once provided a head of water to work the mine water wheels but which is now a reservoir.

1 *From Coniston take the minor road right of the Black Bull.*

2 *The road becomes a mine track. Ascend it.*

A Church Beck. Some impressive waterfalls here after rain.

B Note the rocks' larva-flow patterns and the glacial scratches.

C View of Coniston Old Man's flank. An old chimney of Red Dell mine workings can be seen above the valley right. Close about are the remains of the dressing and washing floors of the mines. In its heyday 200 men were employed here. The Youth Hostel was the mines' office and manager's house.

3 *Go left in front of Youth Hostel and round, following track.*

4 *Follow the track upwards.*

D Underground water tank. An example of unobtrusive engineering.

5 *Do not cross the beck, but double back right on old mine track, then sharp left at elbow to continue the climb to the Levers Water dam.*

6 *Go over the sill. If this is impassable you should walk right round the tarn to the south-eastern end.*

E Simon's Nick. An old mine. DO NOT APPROACH BEYOND FENCE.

7 *There is need to go sharp left after fenced mine shafts above, left. At first the way is obscure over boulders but the path is seen over the grass beyond. Descend on it.*

F 'Boulder Valley'. A 'giants' playground' under awesome crags.

8 *Cross the bridge and continue on.*

G The Pudding Stone. The largest stone of the many.

9 *Head for the quarry plateau and the track beyond it.*

H Below, juniper has colonised the rocky terrain, with a few yews.

10 *T-junction. Go left, then almost immediately left again on descending path.*

I An enclosure here almost completely taken over by juniper.

11 *Bad step! Descend carefully - on your rear end if necessary!*

12 *Keep to the right side of the beck.*

J More views of Church Beck's waterfalls.

13 *Continue on past farm buildings into Coniston.*

Walk 29

HAWKSHEAD MOOR FROM HAWKSHEAD

3½ miles (5.6km) Moderate

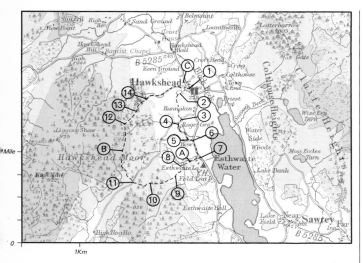

This walk through fields and woodland involves some uphills and some rough paths. It goes through the edge of Grizedale Forest, where there is a view over Esthwaite Water to the Pennines.

Hawkshead is where Wordsworth went to school. The old grammar school is open to the public and is worth a visit, as is the old church which stands above it.

1 *From the village's southern end by the car park, go up past the grammar school and through the churchyard to the end.*

2 *Turn left on the path between fences and follow it through.*

3 *Join the minor road and go right for a short distance.*

4 *Go left between some houses on macadam surface until a slate foot-bridge is reached. Go right across it and follow the fence.*

5 *Go through the gate at the fence end, round the left side of farm, through another gate then go left down the track.*

6 *Join the road and go right.*

7 *Turn right on track (signposted) between buildings and left at the end to join a track ascending by a ravine side.*

A *A pleasant piece of woodland in and about the ravine, mainly ash and beech but some oak and sycamore with typical woodland flora.*

8 *A field is entered; cross the beck, then the path meanders a little to the left of the hill top by a large ash tree.*

9 *At the hill top the path goes through a gateway and follows a wall and*

fence, then curves round a swamp to a rise. Then go right by a fainter green path following a line of trees.

10 *Go through the gates by the cottage (closing them afterwards) and go on the track upwards towards the road.*

11 *Join road, go right, then left up the forest road following it onwards bearing right, ignoring junctions on the left.*

B The forest around here was devastated by the severe gales in the winter of 1983/84 and the tangle of skittled trees was removed by the foresters with great difficulty. On the right the Forestry Commission has left the view open and is restricting the height of intervening plantings. The view is over Esthwaite Water and on a clear day one can see right on to the Yorkshire Pennines. In front as the road is ascended is the High Street range with Wansfell, above Ambleside, before. The Fairfield range is left of this.

12 *Watch right for the forest boundary corner with fields behind. Here take a rough track dropping right to Hawkshead.*

13 *Beware of slippery rock at beck crossing. Go through the gate and descend the rough track.*

14 *Join the macadam lane and follow it down to village.*

C Anne Tyson's Cottage. Here Wordsworth lodged for a while when he was attending the school, before the Tysons moved to Colthouse.

BLACK CRAG

8 miles (12.8km) Strenuous

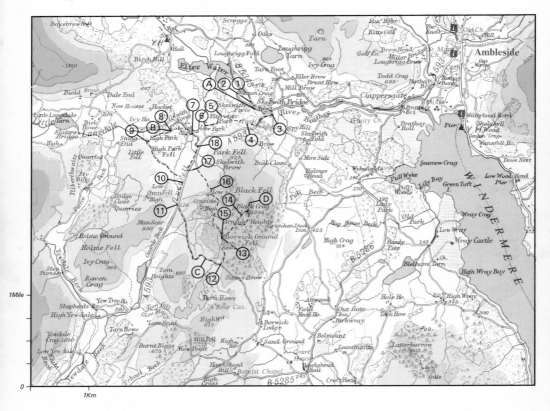

'Black Crag' sounds fearsome and ominous. In fact it is not a very high point, and the prospect presented from its friendly summit is extraordinary. It is arguably among the very best that the Lake District has. It looks into the soft beauty of northern Windermere basins one way, and straight into the drama of the central high fells the other way. Once reached the eminence will tempt a long stay and a leisurely look around. This is a longer walk taking in the two waterfalls at Skelwith and Colwith. The way may be found by some to be testing in parts, with the possibility of a little wetness. The walk also includes part of what is euphemistically called locally 'The Mountain Road' north of Tarn Hows, a very pleasant track.

1 *The walk starts at a car park made in an old quarry near Rob Rash (NT). This is a short way down the road to Langdale from Skelwith Bridge and is on the right.*

2 *Walk from the car park back towards Skelwith Bridge, soon picking up the footpath on the right of the road which goes by Skelwith Force.*

A Skelwith Force. Although the drop of this waterfall is only about 20ft (6m), it takes in a massive flow of water from the Langdale fells and from Wrynose and Little Langdale fells.

3 *The path goes through the quarry Over*

yard and reaches the bridge at Skelwith. Cross the bridge, go right, and pick up the footpath which soon starts on the right. Follow it on.

4 The path passes in front of Park House and inclines right.

5 There is a path junction. The route goes left, by the yard at Elterwater Park and onward.

6 The route goes by Low Park farmhouse, and directly by a stile and through a field by a wooded bank, and across another field to a minor road.

7 Join the road, go right for a short distance, and then left on the footpath for Colwith Falls (NT).

8 Keep by the river side for the falls and take care not to go too close; the rocks can be slippery. Afterwards follow the path on through the woods and leftwards.

B Colwith Force. The view is partly obscured by the deepness of the ravine and the trees cover. The falls in all descend about 70ft (21m). The river is the Brathay which takes a ninety degree turn into Elterwater before reaching Skelwith Force and eventually Windermere.

9 The route goes right and to High Park, joins a minor road and goes left along it.

10 At the road junction go right to follow a footpath over the wall by the roadside, to emerge through trees at a road junction.

11 Cross the road and go up the minor road opposite. This soon becomes a track and begins to climb. This is the 'Mountain Road'.

C There is a view over Tarn Hows at this point.

12 On the left a gate is passed, then an enclosed woodland is approached. Near the top of the track a gap will be seen, and a track leading into the wood with a crag towering on its right. Take this track and follow it upwards to its emergence in moorland at its upper end.

13 Follow the track left for a short distance, then pick up the grassy path going off sharply on the right, following it on to the higher summit point crowned by a triangulation column.

D Black Crag (NT). The northern part of Windermere attracts the eye; to the right of this is Esthwaite Water beyond Hawkshead, and closer by Tarn Hows. But here too is a 'balcony' view of the central fells. Coniston Water is to the south-west and the Coniston Old Man range is close, with its large north-eastern spur, Wetherlam, prominent. To the right of this is Little Langdale and Wrynose, then Crinkle Crags are visible and Pike o' Blisco. If the air is clear Scafell Pike, the highest point in England, 3210ft (978m) might be made out peeping just to the right of this. Then nearer is Bowfell, at Great Langdale's head. Great End, on the Scafell Pikes range, might be seen right of Bowfell, then the Langdale Pikes. Way up to the north is Saddleback, some 16 miles (25.7km) away. To the right of this, the Helvellyn range is seen end on, then crowded to the right with the Fairfield range. To the right is Kirkstone Pass and the High Street range, also seen end on. To vary the view go down to the lower cairned summit. The tarn below is Blelham.

14 Follow the path back to rejoin the track at the high end of the wood.

15 This time turn right and follow the track on and down. Ignore the left turning and go past Low Arnside.

16 Junction. Go left.

17 Junction. Go left to the road then follow the road on right with care.

18 Road junction. Go left, descending to the hill foot to pick up the footpath across the field by the riverside, returning by the same paths as the outward route, to Skelwith and Rob Rash.

Walk 31
WRAY AND LATTERBARROW
4 miles (6.5km) Strenuous

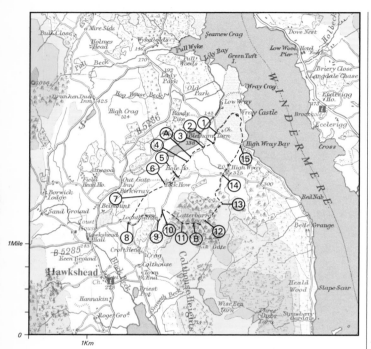

The climb to the superb viewpoint of Latterbarrow between Hawkshead and Windermere was described in *Walk the Lakes*. This is another walk taking in this summit and walking about it on paths around the Wray Castle Estate (NT). Much of it is on farmland paths, and the finish is through forest and by Windermere's shore.

1 The walk starts by the gateway into the grounds of Wray Castle, a Victorian eccentricity. There are a few places near the gate where cars can be parked, otherwise there is a car park down the drive behind the castle.

Walk southwards, deviating from the road right, by fence, for a view over to Langdale Pikes. This rejoins the road.

2 Go right on footpath (signed). Follow the fence on the left and on to the footbridge and across it.

3 Go through the trees and follow the path on the field edges through two stiles, then path veers right.

A A view of Blelham Tarn and bog, a National Nature Reserve.

4 A stile leads onto a track by an ancient ash, and goes on past the farm to a macadam lane.

5 Go onwards on lane and right on path (signed Hawkshead).

6 Follow path round field corner, through gate and left with wall for a short distance, then incline right on a low ridge and across a hollow to stile. (There should be route marks.)

7 Cross the ditch by the fence then go leftwards to old gate-posts, then follow a line of trees, by stile and hedge to the farm and minor road.

8 Follow the minor road leftwards to join another road.

9 Go left on the road for a short distance.

10 Go right for Latterbarrow (signed).

11 Take any of the footpaths which lead to the summit.

B Latterbarrow. The views are extensive. Over to the northwest are the unmistakable peaks of Langdale Pikes. Skiddaw should be seen to the north and right of that and nearer, the Helvellyn range. Then nearer again is the Fairfield range with Kirkstone Pass visible on the right. Westwards is the Cóniston Old Man range.

12 From the summit descend northeastwards with the head of Windermere in view to pick up a path which eventually leads down to a stile onto a forest road.

13 Turn left along the forest road and track into the village.

14 Bear right, through village, then right at the end on a footpath down to the lake shore.

15 Follow the path by the shore and up by Wray Castle to start.

Walk 32
APPLETHWAITE COMMON
4 miles (6.4km) Easy

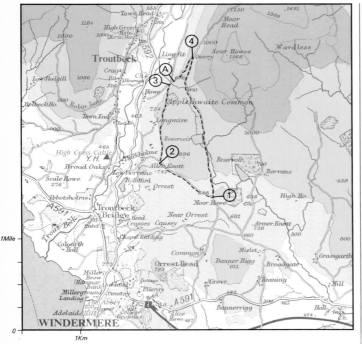

This easy walk is on by-road and tracks and one can walk it dry-shod.

1 *The walk starts from a by-road between Troutbeck and Ings. To find the start point from Windermere go along the Kendal road (A591) from Windermere station, take the first turning left, cross a junction, go to the T-junction, go left and stop by a track junction, right. There is a wide splay at this place. Parking is possible without obstructing. Having parked, walk down the road towards Troutbeck.*

2 *At the first junction turn right along the by-way and follow it straight on.*

3 *At the junction keep right and ascend.*

A Viewpoint over Troutbeck valley. Troutbeck village is spread along the hillside opposite. The church is below the village, which seems odd, but it serves a scattered community of which the village is only part. The village is in fact a collection of tiny hamlets each grouped around wells named after saints: St John's, St Margaret's, St James'. Many of the houses date back to the 17th and 18th centuries. At the southern end (on the left) is Town End. The 17th-century house there, carefully preserved, is in the care of The National Trust and open to the public. It provides a fascinating insight into the history and way of life of the close community. It is well worth a visit. Above Town End a tree-lined lane may be seen contouring round the fell side, a way to Ambleside. Does this follow the old Roman road which must have come down the Troutbeck valley from the High Street fells on the route from Brougham fort to Ambleside's fort? The village inn, the Mortal Man, existed in the 17th century but was 'improved' and enlarged in the 19th century. The old legend on the inn sign remains:

'Oh mortal man that lives by bread
What is it makes thy face so red?
Oh silly ass that looks so pale,
'Tis from drinking Sally Birkett's ale.'

4 *At the junction with the upper path, turn right along it and continue on to start.*

Walk 33
BEATRIX POTTER WALK
6 miles (8km) Moderate

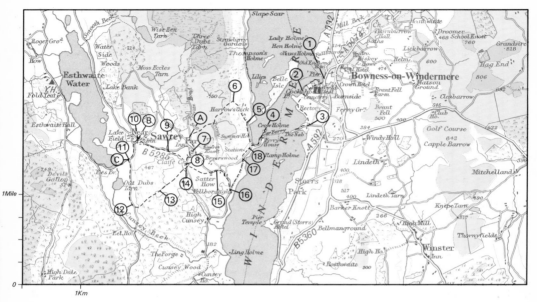

Beatrix Potter's cottage, Hill Top (NT), is at Near Sawrey, south-east of Hawkshead. It is one of the most visited houses in the country. The problem is that it is so small and that the numbers wanting to see it are so great. Most people drive there and find that they have great difficulty in finding somewhere to put their car. Often it is impossible to park in the tiny village. A large car park would ruin it and result in a crush of visitors anyway that could not be accommodated. So here described is a walk to the cottage from Bowness. It is not the shortest way, but it avoids most of the narrow road traffic hazards of going direct and goes through pleasant country largely unaltered since Beatrix Potter's days. Many of her illustrations were done in the area. (N.B. Hill Top is closed on Fridays and on Sunday mornings.)

1 *From Bowness pier, walk south-west past the Information Centre and the main car park.*

2 *Keeping straight on, go through the iron gate and by the footpath round by the lake shore to the ferry road.*

3 *Turn right and embark on the ferry.*

4 *From the ferry walk along the road and pick up the footpath (signed) on the right. This goes past the Ferry House complex and cuts the corner onto the lake-side minor road.*

5 *After a quarter of a mile a cattle grid is reached. A footpath leaves it, left, to climb the hill through a wood.*

6 *A cross track is reached. Go up left and follow this track all the way, ignoring branch paths.*

A Here is the first view over the Sawreys, Beatrix Potter country.

7 *The track finishes at Far Sawrey. Turn right along the road and go first left down a minor road towards the church.*

8 *Go right, through the kissing gate and on the path diagonally across the field, then go right by a beck to a kissing gate onto the road.*

9 *Go left along the road side to Near Sawrey and Hill Top.*

B Near Sawrey. Beatrix Potter had known Near Sawrey since 1896. Her parents rented a house here (now called Eeswyke). When she found herself with a little capital she bought Hill Top farm in 1905 to realise a long held wish. She kept on the tenant, John Cannon, as her *Over* farm manager, building a wing for him to occupy and adding a dairy. She kept the old farmhouse for her own use. Though she loved it dearly, she did not intend to live there permanently, but spent several weeks at a time there when she was able. During the eight years of owning and enjoying Hill Top she was at her most productive, writing and illustrating some thirteen books. As she began to prosper she bought up more property in the village and in 1913 married the solicitor who had been acting for her in the purchases, William Heelis. Hill Top was too small for them and they lived in another cottage by Castle Farm nearby. After her marriage, her writing activity diminished as she took a consuming interest in farming. One of the rumours about her which was once voiced was that she disliked children. Villagers who knew her deny this vigorously, but the rumour persists.

Beatrix Potter rarely painted the fascinating scenery in her books from memory. It was all painted on site. Some stories were set in Borrowdale, Newlands, Derwentwater, Hawkshead and Little Langdale, and a few outside the Lake District; but quite a number of scenes, still identifiable, are around Hill Top and Near Sawrey. The Tower Bank Arms (NT) and the fields behind Hill Top are in *The Tale of Jemima Puddleduck*. Buckle Yeat, on the Hawkshead side of the Tower Bank, and other local cottages are illustrated in *The Pie and the Patty Pan*. The post office in the same book can be seen across the field opposite Hill Top. The lane leading off the road opposite the Tower Bank is in *The Tale of Jeremy Fisher* and *The Tale of Tom Kitten*, and the same lane viewed from the roof of Hill Top is in *The Tale of Samuel Whiskers*. The shop in *The Tale of Ginger and Pickles* used to be opposite Anvil House. But lots of other illustrations are gleaned from the atmosphere of this lovely area, the woods, and the rocks, and the wild flowers.

10 *From Hill Top walk on towards Hawkshead, then take the turning left down the minor road.*

11 *Keep left at the junction and go straight on.*

C Road junction. This is illustrated in *The Tale of Pigling Bland*. Only the modern road sign intrudes on the scene from the original: the trees and walls are the same. Further along the walk, the bluebell wood in *The Fairy Caravan* is over the wall to the left. A view over Esthwaite Water can be seen if desired, by going a few yards right down the lane. Such a view was in *The Tale of Jeremy Fisher*.

12 *At the end of the field left, go left over stiles into the wood. The track goes left shortly after entering and then meanders upwards. Avoid branch paths left. The track finishes by curving right, by a fence and then goes left with it to a stile into a field.*

13 *The path crosses field then goes by stiles and gates along a terraced track to a kissing gate and a minor road.*

14 *Go left, then go right on the footpath by the church's side.*

15 *The path finishes at the road by cottages. Go right along the road for a short distance, then right down minor road.*

16 *Take the lane left to walk by the lake shore.*

17 *The lane finishes at the road. Cross it, go through the little car park, and walk along the footpath through the wood which runs parallel with the road.*

18 *The path joins the road. Follow the road on right, to the ferry and the return to Bowness.*

Walk 34
BRANT FELL AND SCHOOL KNOTT
5 miles (8km) Easy

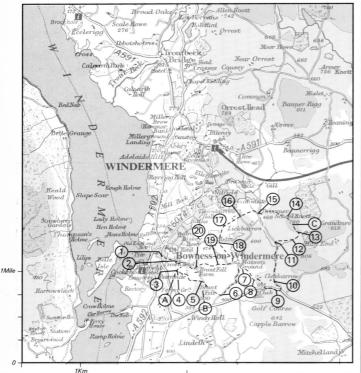

Caught up in the hurly-burly of Bowness-on-Windermere in the height of the season it might be hard to believe that in a short distance up the higher land to the east there is a delightful quiet country area offering some lovely views; yet these public rights of way are not often walked. This route is recommended.

1 *The walk starts at St Martin's Square in Bowness, which is opposite the church. On the east side (farthest from the church) a road goes south (A5074) but from this Brantfell Road goes left up the hill. Follow this to the top.*

2 *At the end of the road go on by the path up the grassy hill. At the hill top go right with the fences, and then round the terraced path.*

3 *Go right, through the gate, to the view point.*

A Post Knott (NT). The view here is down the lake's lower reaches.

4 *Go back to the gate but do not go through it. Go right with the wall, over the stile in the corner and onwards, following the wall.*

5 *Join the track and follow it, ignoring*

tractor track right. However, divert right to Brant Fell viewpoint. N.B. There is no right of way here. The owner permits access. (After visit return to track.)

B Brant Fell. Here again the best view from the rocky summit is down the wooded banks of Windermere. A pleasant spot to linger.

6 *At the track end go over the stile onto the minor road, and go left on it to just past Matson Ground.*

7 *Go right by the footpath (signed) and on through the gates.*

8 *A drive is joined, go right on it to the road.*

9 *Go left along the road side (with care!) then go left soon along the drive by Cleabarrow.*

10 *Go straight on along the track through the gates.*

11 *The fell is approached. Do not go first right by the tractor track. Go on further to pick up a prominent stony track on the right.*

12 *Ignore the turning right through the wall gap. Carry straight on, following the wall to the tarn.*

13 *Walk alongside the tarn for a short distance then go left to climb to the summit.*

C School Knott. The view is a pleasant surprise. The lake is below, though partly obscured by foreground, but the central fells appear in their glory. Prominent on the right are the Langdale Pikes. Just left of the left-hand pike (Pike o' Stickle), if the air is clear, can be seen the peak of Great Gable over 15 miles (24km) away. Great End on the Scafell Pike range is just left of *Over* that and then, before it, left again, is the bulk of Bow Fell with its peak on the left. Left again and 14 miles (22.5km) away is Scafell Pike, the highest point in England. The crinkles of Crinkle Crags are left again and forward, and left of that is the Coniston Old Man range.

14 *Head down towards Windermere (direction of Langdale Pikes) ignoring turning right, but heading for the stile. Do not go over the stile, but go left through the gate and on briefly.*

15 *Watch for some steps down right to a footbridge. Cross it and by stile and then go left with the walls.*

16 *Join the road and go by the footpath signed opposite.*

17 *The path curves round to a path junction. Go left alongside fence going left to Helm Farm.*

18 *Helm Farm junction. Go on through the stile and follow the hedge on the left. Go through a stile and*

bear right by the houses. Follow the wall on the right and look for a kissing gate in it and go right and by tarmac lane.

19 *Go right for a few yards, then bear left by a fence through a gate and onwards.*

20 *Cross the drive to the farm, go on through the gate and down to the start.*

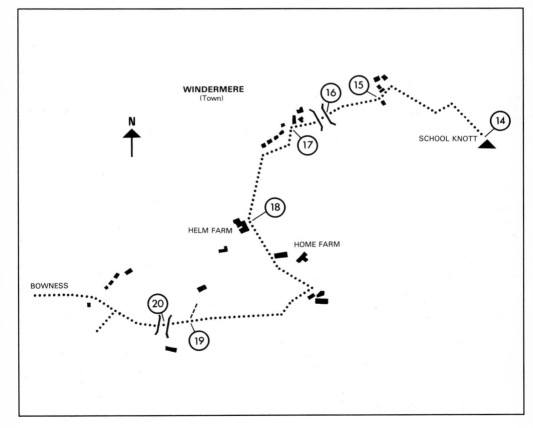

ADELAIDE HILL
3½ miles (5.6km) Easy

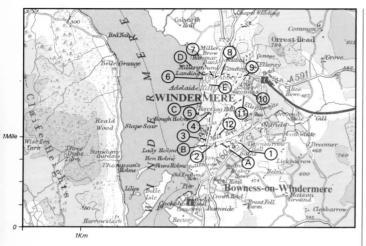

This walk from Windermere town goes by old cottages and woodland to the lake shore and a viewpoint hill. It can be linked with a visit to the unique Steamboat Museum which it passes.

1 *The walk starts at a bus stop/lay-by opposite Thornbarrow Road in Windermere town, just north of the Police Station. Walk westwards towards the lake on the footpath (signed).*

A Millbeck. A diversion right to the beck reveals a pretty waterfall. Although old cottages are soon seen, the mill has gone.

2 *The path crosses a track and descends past cottages to road.*

B The Steamboat Museum. The museum houses a remarkable collection of some of the oldest steam vessels in the world, from the elegant to the eminently practical.

Occasional cruises are a feature.

3 *Walk northwards along the road side.*

4 *After two entrances (to hall and farm) a footpath (signed) is taken left for the lake shore across a field.*

5 *Join the lake shore path and follow it to the right.*

C Adelaide Tree. The observant may find a metal plaque in an old sycamore tree recording the fact that Queen Adelaide landed there in July 1840. Adelaide of Saxe Meiningen was queen to William IV. In 1840 she had been widowed for three years. Victoria was queen.

6 *There is a choice here is of continuing on lake shore, but if the lake level prevents this there is a stile right, through wall to a path which rejoins the shore further on.*

D Millerground. Hereabouts was the corn mill. Records show that it was in production in 1535. The cot-

tage is one of the oldest in the area - early 17th-century. The bell turret on the adjoining building might puzzle. In fact from this point a ferry used to ply across the lake to Belle Grange opposite, to link up with an old road to Hawkshead. The ferryman could be summoned from the far side by a pull on the bell rope.

7 *Follow the path upwards by the beck side to the top, then turn right to ascend the green hill - Adelaide Hill.*

E Adelaide Hill (NT). This was so named to honour the queen's visit. The excellent view includes a good part of the lake, Wetherlam on the left, then Crinkle Crags and Bowfell, then the Langdale Pikes are seen at their best. Further right is the Fairfield range, with Red Screes right, then Thornthwaite and Ill Bell on High Street.

8 *Cross the road with care and go up the (signed) footpath almost opposite left. Follow it up all the way.*

9 *The main road is joined but only for a few yards. Go right to join the footpath going right just before the church.*

10 *The path goes left, past some old cottages. After this take the footpath leaving on the right.*

11 *A minor road is joined. Cross it and go down the unclassified road/track opposite left. After the houses are passed it becomes a pleasant track through woodlands.*

12 *The track reaches the point where the footpath crosses from the starting point. Ascend left.*

Walk 36
STAVELEY WALK
6 miles (9.6km) Strenuous

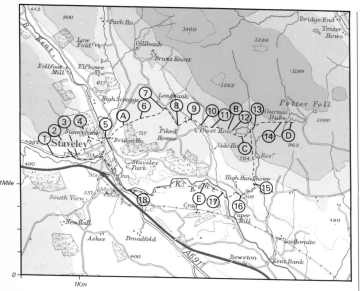

Staveley, until it gets its much needed by-pass, is on the A591, half way between Kendal and Windermere. The walk described climbs from the village to the tarns which have been impounded to take water for the village's paper mill. The farther one, Gurnal Dubbs, is attractive notwithstanding, set in open moorland. The walk returns by the banks of the River Kent.

1 Parking is impossible in Staveley. There is a quarry lay-by half a mile to the west. Park here. Walkers coming by public transport should alight at Staveley and walk up the Kentmere road to Barley Bridge (point 5 in directions).

2 Take minor road into the village from the west (Brow Lane).

3 Take first turning left, signed 'Crag End'. Go up following the wall. Cross the stile and go right to next stile.

4 At Sunny Bank (house) take path by it on right. Follow wall right and bend right between walls to join road and bridge.

5 Barley Bridge. Cross it, go right for a few yards, then left upwards between buildings. Go through gate and follow wall and fence left uphill. This path is not too obvious.

A Birkhag Wood. There is a good view here of the Kentmere valley.

6 The path veers away from wall. Watch for step stile right. Follow the wall on the left downhill. Then follow another wall down to the house.

7 Go past the house to the road and turn right along it.

8 Take the first turning left towards Birk Field buildings.

9 At the buildings go right then left in front of the cottage, lane then bends right following stream.

10 Path bends left and goes upwards by plantation to a track.

11 Cross the track and go upwards on the same line on an obscure path marked initially by a few cairns. Watch the wall on the right as the path eventually goes through it.

B Viewpoint north-westwards to most of the central fells.

12 Go over a stone step stile in a bend on the wall and onwards to Potter Tarn.

C Potter Tarn. Pretty but artificial and an unlovely dam.

13 A path will be seen going up the fell from near the spillway. Take this. It meanders and reaches Gurnal Dubbs.

D Gurnal Dubbs. Two tarns dammed to make one. The setting here is inviting among grass and heather. A place to rest and enjoy.

14 Return to Potter Tarn by the same route. Then descend the track all the way.

15 At junction go right. After joining minor road go right.

16 By farm go left down to the river and cross the bridge.

17 Follow the river bank path by stiles and gates all the way.

E The beginning of the riverside walk is very attractive.

18 Path eventually joins roadside. Walk back to start.

Walk 37
SCOUT SCAR AND HELSINGTON
5½ miles (9km) Moderate

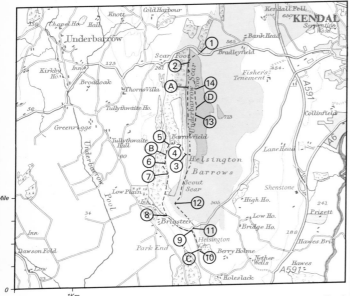

During the Carboniferous period of geological time some 300 million years ago, the Lake District, like most of Britain, was covered by a warm sea. The deposits of mud and debris included the skeletons of myriads of sea animals. This material eventually became sedimentary lime-rich rock and it covered the Lake District in parts up to more than half a mile (0.8km) thick. The great glaciers of the Ice Age followed by the great erosive floods scoured most of the limestone away. None of it remains in the central Lake District. It is in evidence around the rim. The buildings of Kendal and Grange over Sands are largely limestone. To the west of Kendal, south-moving ice and flood swept out deeply what is now the

Lyth valley, leaving a great wall of near vertical rock — a sort of limestone Wast Water Screes. This is Underbarrow Scar, with Scout Scar at its southern end. It offers a remarkable and exhilarating view of the Lake District, and a delightful airy walk. In spring the limestone is of special interest to botanists. This walk goes the length of the scar, with views nearly all the way. It goes through Honeybee Wood and visits one of the best-sited churches in the Lake District: a happy setting hanging over the delectable Lyth valley. An atheist would find it inspiring.

1 *The walk starts from Scout Scar car park (NP) which is two miles east of Kendal on the Underbarrow road. Approaching from Kendal the car*

park is just over the brow of the hill, on the right. Cross the road from the car park, go right a few paces, then left through the iron gate to follow the path up the hill.

2 *Walk along the cliff edge footpath.*
A Viewpoints all the way along, to the Lyth valley below, the central fells to the north-west, and Morecambe Bay ahead. The tree growth on the crags below is notable. The trees have to withstand strong turbulent winds and have grown accordingly to fit their environment. Limestone rocks are favoured by yew trees and there are some wind-moulded specimens. But a dominant tree here is the whitebeam, the tree with white undersides to its leaves. It is a Sorbus, close relative to the mountain ash, and it is quite at home in this situation. Whitebeam is a tough wood and was used by millers to make cogs for the wooden cog wheels. It is still used to make tool handles.

On the plateau, too, the tree growth is remarkable considering that this, too, is a difficult environment, for trees have not only to cope with rocky terrain and shallow soil, but sheep grazing. Here ash trees are the main survivors, with some hawthorns.

3 *As the walk continues along the cliff, it passes a ruined wall and a farm can be seen below. The way passes the farm and the footpath to it is found after the farm below has been passed and there is a dip in the ridge. The path doubles back and descends through a wood.*

Over

4 *At the gate at the foot of the path and edge of the wood go straight across the field to go through the gates to the left of the farm.*

5 *Go left on the track into Honeybee Wood.*

B Honeybee Wood. One could hardly imagine a more diverse mixture of trees in this delightful wood in the care of the Forestry Commission. The only obvious aliens in the mass of hardwoods are some cypress trees.

6 *The track leaves the wood at a cattle grid. The right of way here goes right onto a narrow woodland path running parallel with the track.*

7 *The path turns to the track again. Strictly speaking, the right of way continues through the woodland, again parallel with the track. However it can be such a jungle that it might prove prudent to accept the Forestry Commission's hospitality and use their track. Follow it through to the end.*

8 *Join the road and go up it steeply to the left.*

9 *Near the top of the hill turn right to Helsington Church.*

C St John's Church, Helsington. The church itself dates only from 1726 though it is possibly on the site of an earlier chapel. The name 'Helsington' suggests an Anglian settlement. Its glory is its aspect. The Wordsworth lines quoted at the gate are apt:

> 'The very angels whose
>   authentic lays,
> Sung from that ground in
>   middle air,
> Made known the spot where
>   piety should raise
> A holy structure to the
>   Almighty's praise.'

A mural on the east wall by Marion D'Aumaret (1920) picks up this theme.

It is a site which compels one to linger. Below is the Lyth valley and it seems obvious from here that the valley was once a great wide river which swept out this valley between this spot and the ridge opposite: Whitbarrow Scar. The relatively puny River Gilpin and its tributary the River Pool below are all that remain of the great flood. Gilpin is joined by the River Kent from Kentmere through Kendal. It is hard to believe now perhaps, but early last century from here one would be able to see ships coming in with the tide to the port of Milnthorpe. One of the valuable cargoes coming in was saltpetre and sulphur for the gunpowder mills at Sedgwick, south of Kendal, and Elterwater. Any hope of the village continuing as a port was ended by the building of the railway viaduct at Arnside which hastened the silting up of Milnthorpe sands.

10 *Return to the road, and turn right for a short way.*

11 *Turn left into The National Trust's Helsington Barrows (signed). Follow the path on through the gate.*

12 *The path turns right to join the Scout Scar cliff walk.*

13 *Turn aside to visit 'the mushroom' viewpoint.*

D 'The mushroom'. The diagram around the ceiling, if it is still legible, will settle any disagreements you might have had on identifying the distant fells. Most prominent to the west is the Coniston Old Man range as the whole flank is exposed from Dow Crag at its southern end to Wetherlam at its northern. To the right is Crinkle Crags, and Scafell Pike might be seen peeping over the left shoulder of Bowfell at the head of Langdale, with Great Gable at its other shoulder. The Pikes of Langdale follow.

14 *Continue onwards to join the path back to the road and the start.*

Reference:
Wordsworth W. 'Engelberg, the Hill of Angels' from *Tour on the Continent 1820.*

Walk 38

WINSTER

5 miles (8km) Strenuous

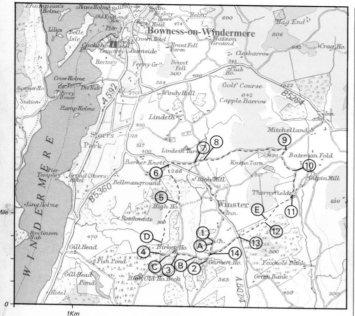

round the end of the barn left, and up the green lane.

C Signs of bank and ditch, left, are indications of ancient forest.

4 T-junction. Go right on a track.

D Just after a gate there is a fine view of the fells left. Coniston Old Man range is nearest, the Langdale Fells to the right. As the path takes a turn right, the Fairfield horseshoe and the High Street range come into view.

5 The main track swings right. The way lies left before reaching the gate. It follows a wall on the path's right.

6 The path reaches the road. **CROSS WITH CARE - BLIND BEND LEFT.** Go up the lane opposite.

7 Cross the minor road.

8 Go up the lane signed 'Green Lane'. It starts as macadam and goes green after driveways leave it on the right and left.

9 Join the minor road, go right, and then first left.

10 Junction. Continue right.

11 Go to the right of the barn to pick up a green track.

E Bow Mabble Breast. An odd name for the oak-covered ridge, right.

12 The green path meanders, but general direction continues.

13 *IMPORTANT. THESE GATES MUST BE SECURED.* Go through gate, cross the road with care, and go through the gate opposite. Follow the field wall and join a green track between walls.

14 The track joins the road; turn right for the starting point.

Before the main roads were improved and transport made easier, the countryside was served with a network of lanes, some of them well engineered. Many of these are now only paths and bridleways, but are pleasant to use as their makers had an eye for taking the best line. This walk around Winster uses these old lanes among scenery that is typically British rather than Lake District: meadows, trees, rocks and valleys. The way undulates so there is climbing.

1 Start the walk at the lay-by by

Winster's church. This is reached from Winster village on the A5074 from Bowness, from a road opposite the Brown Horse Inn signed 'Bowland Bridge'.

A Holy Trinity Church. Attraction is tranquillity not antiquity.

2 Southwards from the church, take the first turning to the right, a driveway serving two houses and a public footpath.

B The scene here is eye-pleasing, a near perfect blend of green field, woods, and two fine old houses with rising land behind.

3 Go right on the lane before the house,